INTRODUCING

Buddha

Jane Hope and Borin Van Loon

Edited by Richard Appignanesi

ICON BOOKS UK   TOTEM BOOKS USA

This edition published in the UK
in 1999 by Icon Books Ltd.,
Grange Road, Duxford,
Cambridge CB2 4QF
email: icon@mistral.co.uk
www.iconbooks.co.uk

Distributed in the UK, Europe,
Canada, South Africa and Asia by the
Penguin Group: Penguin Books Ltd.,
27 Wrights Lane, London W8 5TZ

This edition published in Australia
in 1999 by Allen & Unwin Pty. Ltd.,
PO Box 8500, 9 Atchison Street,
St. Leonards NSW 2065

Previously published in the UK in 1994
and Australia in 1995 under the title
Buddha for Beginners

Reprinted 1995, 1996, 1998

First published in the United States
in 1995 by Totem Books
Inquiries to: PO Box 223,
Canal Street Station,
New York, NY 10013

Reprinted 1998

In the United States,
distributed to the trade by
National Book Network Inc.,
4720 Boston Way, Lanham,
Maryland 20706

Library of Congress Catalog
Card Number: 95–060973

Originating editor: Richard Appignanesi

Printed and bound in Australia
by McPherson's Printing Group, Victoria

«To study the way of Buddha is to study oneself. To study oneself is to forget oneself. To forget oneself is to be enlightened by everything in the world. To be enlightened by everything is to surrender one's own body & mind.»

PART ONE

INTRODUCTION

There is much misunderstanding about who or what the Buddha was. The word Buddha literally means "awakened one".

Eastern traditions recognize that there have been many buddhas in the past and will be many buddhas in the future.

Nevertheless, there was a historical figure, whose family name was Siddhartha Gautama, and who has become known as the Buddha for this age. He was also known as Sakyamuni Buddha, the sage of the Sakyas. The life and teachings of the historical Buddha are a milestone in human understanding, but the Buddha himself was an ordinary man with no claims to divine origin. Belief in a creator God has no part in the Buddhist religion.

In the Buddhist lineage, knowledge is not handed down like an antique. One teacher experiences the truth of the teachings and hands it down as inspiration to his students. That inspiration wakens the student who passes it on further. The teachings are seen as always up to date, they are not thought of as "ancient wisdom".

It is like a recipe for bread. Each baker must apply his general knowledge of how to bake bread, but each time it is cooked it is completely fresh.

5

WAS THE BUDDHA AN HISTORICAL FIGURE?

The doctrine of change and impermanence which is at the heart of Buddhism constantly breaks up any tendencies towards fundamentalism.

The Buddhist experience relies on experiencing the truth for oneself, and ultimately it does not really matter whether or not there was an historical Buddha. However, the traditions and legends that surround the life of the Buddha contain in allegorical form, the precise nature and form of the spiritual journey.

The early stories and teachings of the Buddha were not written down until several centuries after his death. They were not seen as the "authorized version". The Buddha encouraged his followers to put everything he said to the test, and therefore, through the ages, followers of the Buddha have trusted their own wisdom, rather than trying to interpret what might have been meant in old texts.

THE LIFE OF THE BUDDHA

Prince Siddartha was born around 560BC in a small kingdom just below the Himalayan foothills. His father was a king of the Sakya clan. His mother, Queen Maya was said to be so radiant and alluring that even the gods envied her. She was called Mayadevi "Goddess of Illusion" because her body was so beautiful as to be unbelievable. On the night of the Buddha's conception, Queen Maya dreamed that a white elephant had entered her womb. The dream revealed to her that the child would be special.

Soon after Siddartha was born, a holy man prophesied:

If he stays in the palace he could become an outstanding world leader, but if he enters the religious life he will become enlightened, a teacher of gods and men.

This fills me with apprehension! ... I want Siddharta to take over the throne of the kingdom when I die.

IFE IN THE PALACE

The king therefore determined to make the first prediction come true and lavished care and attention on his son. As the prince grew up, he mastered the traditional arts and sciences, becoming skilled in

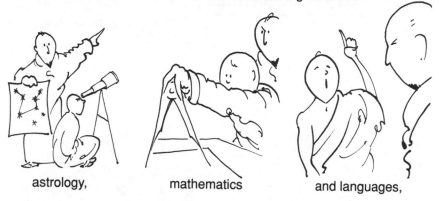

astrology,   mathematics   and languages,

as well as taking part in traditional sports such as

archery,   wrestling   and horsemanship.

It will be the hard facts of life that will turn my son's mind towards religion, so I'll provide every pleasure and luxury that the world can offer!

In order to keep him addicted to the palace, the king had a chamber of love built, decorated with erotic art. Pleasure girls, skilled in the art of love were invited to the palace. Siddartha's life in the palace revolved around the pleasures of the senses.

In the course of time, the palace women told him about the world outside the palace and how beautiful it was. Plans were made for the prince to make a journey, but first the King ordered that anyone who was old or sick or crazy or diseased should be cleared from the roads.

OUTSIDE THE PALACE

The Prince went out of the palace several times, and each time he left, he saw something which disturbed his mind. The first time he saw an old, bent, toothless man.

> Now I realize how old age destroys memory and beauty and strength.

The second time he saw a diseased man with a swollen belly covered with filth and flies.

> Now I realise how the body decays.

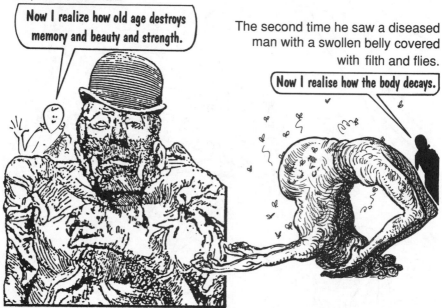

On the third visit, he saw a corpse being carried through the streets, followed by anguished friends and family.

He himself felt frightened and alarmed when he reflected on the inevitability of old age, sickness and death.   He became silent and withdrawn.

The King saw his despair.

The young men rode out together in the beautiful countryside.

I feel estranged from their company. Everywhere I look I see suffering.

He had lost all sense of the intoxication that comes from a pride in being young and vital and strong.

Withdrawing from his good friends, he went to a solitary spot and sat at the foot of a rose-apple tree. There, he reflected on what he had seen. He directly confronted his fear of death and saw the possibility of achieving composure.

Later, Siddartha met a saddhu or holy man on the road.

THE QUEST FOR ENLIGHTENMENT

Siddartha determined not to return to the palace,

he bade his wife and child a silent farewell

and went to the edge of the forest where he cut off his hair with a sword

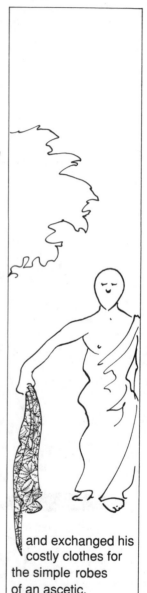

and exchanged his costly clothes for the simple robes of an ascetic. His quest for enlightenment had begun.

From then onwards the prince studied the various systems practised among the ascetics and yogins.

We believe that it is necessary to subjugate the body in order that the mind should be free.

These ascetics are as dedicated to pain as the inhabitants of the palace are to pleasure. They survive on roots, berries, tree bark and water. If they dress at all, it is in rags, and they sleep out in the open or in caves or trees.

They mortified themselves in various ways, as they still do in India today, never bathing, locking themselves permanently into one posture, sitting submerged in mud.

Siddartha's intensity caused him to go further.

I vow to gain complete control over my body and mind by ridding myself of all passions, physical and mental.

He suppressed all thought, stopped his breathing for periods of time and starved his body. At the end of his fast he was reduced to a skeleton and collapsed by the side of the river bank. The village children thought he was a dust demon, but he slowly regained consciousness and washed himself in the river.

A village girl brought him some milk and rice and he ate it with gratitude.

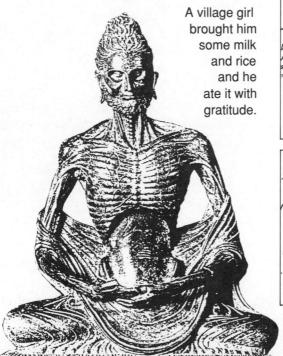

Now that the strength is returning to my body, I see that the path I've been following has led to nothing.

The excessive self-torture has merely worn out my body.

He remembered the insight which came to him as he sat under the rose-apple tree, refreshed, wakeful and without struggle.

Siddartha prepared a comfortable seat of kusha grass underneath a large sheltering tree, known as the Bodhi tree.

I vow that I will not leave this place until my understanding is complete ... Or I die.

He had studied all the sacred texts and tried all the methods. Now there was nothing to rely on, no one to turn to, nowhere to go.

OBSTACLES

It is said that the world rejoiced because of Siddartha's determination to seek freedom, but this aroused the anger of Mara. As well as being an embodiment of death, Mara symbolizes all the obstacles that prevent one from attaining enlightenment.

Traditional descriptions are colourful. "Mara ordered his army to attack Siddhartha with spears of copper, flaming swords and cauldrons of boiling oil. They came riding decaying corpses, and lashing out with hooks and whips and spiked wheels of fire. Some sprouted flames from every hair or rode mad elephants through the tree tops. The earth shook and the regions of space flashed flames. Yet whenever anything touched him, it turned into a rain of flowers, fragrant and soft to the touch."

When the weapons of fear failed to interfere with his equanimity, Mara sent his daughters

to seduce Siddhartha, using all the weapons of seduction. They conjured up a host of goddesses. Traditional descriptions are equally colourful. "Some of the goddesses veiled only half their face; some displayed their full, round breasts; some teased him with half smiles; some stretched and yawned seductively; some deliberately appeared dishevelled; some sighed deeply with passion; some undressed slowly before him, some fingered their golden girdles; some swayed their hips like palm trees. And all whispered to him:

Come and taste the delights of the world and forget about nirvana and the path of liberation until you are old.

He was equally unmoved by desire and saw the ravishing daughters and their phantasmic goddesses in the form of sad old women.

21

Mara and his daughters are familiar to anyone who practises meditation; the revelation of dark repressed fears, barely remembered fragments of memory, doubts, erotic fantasy and foremost, the desire to get back to familiar ground.

SIDDARTHA'S ENLIGHTENMENT

Persisting in this way, his mind became clear and still.

In the first watch of the night, he remembered the successive series of his previous births and thought with compassion:

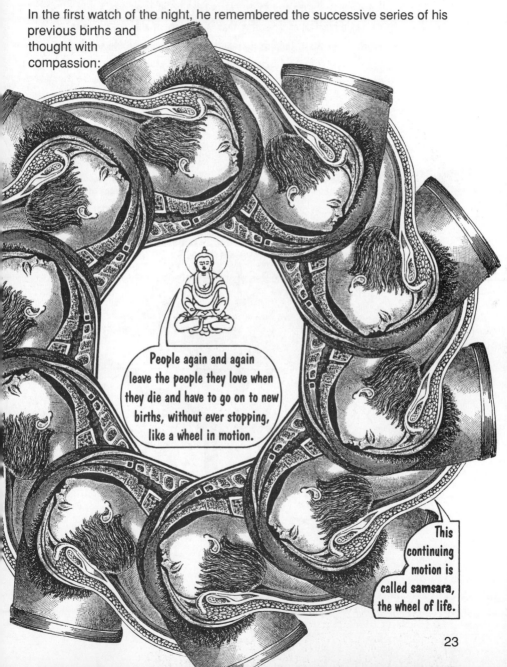

People again and again leave the people they love when they die and have to go on to new births, without ever stopping, like a wheel in motion.

This continuing motion is called **samsara**, the wheel of life.

In the second watch of the night, he saw that people's present experience was caused by their previous actions.

This is called **karma**. Karma originates from a false belief in an ego, which prompts a chain reaction of defending that false sense of self and trying to maintain some security. However, there is no security anywhere and people can find no resting place. There is nothing substantial in the world of samsara.

In the third watch of the night, Siddartha saw ...

People are ignorant of their true nature, and that ignorance causes them to suffer over and over again.

I too have been caught up in the same mechanical process. The being which I believed in was a fictional construction! I have a name, a personal history, memories, thoughts, emotions, dreams; but when I look they are quite illusory. What I have been looking for has never been lost, either to me or to anyone else. There is nothing to attain and no longer any struggle to attain it. The projections of my mind are in essence empty. It is like a raindrop merging into the vastness of the ocean. Or like a cloud disappearing in the sky, arising from space and dissolving into space.

When Siddhartha had this realization, he touched the ground:

I call the Earth to witness my release from the round of birth and death!

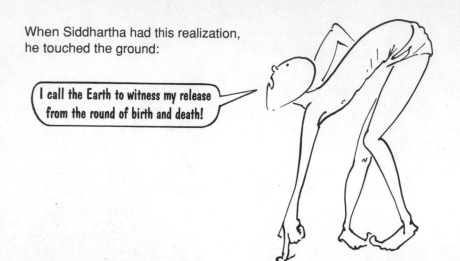

It was said that the earth swayed like a woman drunken with wine and that flowers showered from the sky.

THE BUDDHA

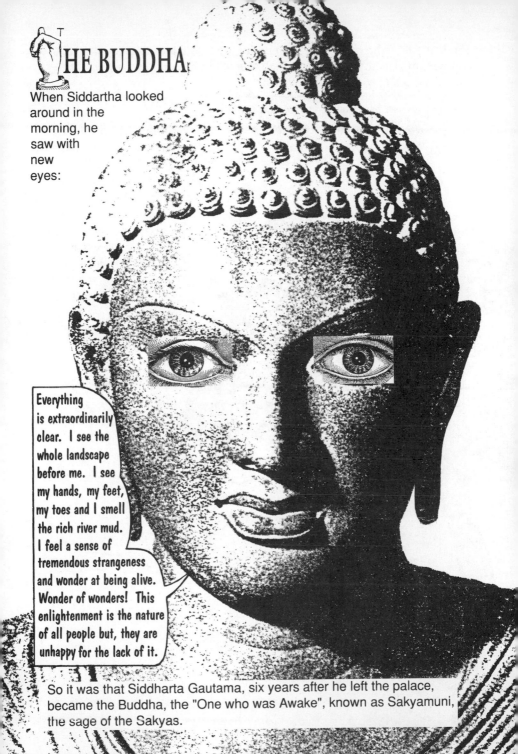

When Siddartha looked around in the morning, he saw with new eyes:

Everything is extraordinarily clear. I see the whole landscape before me. I see my hands, my feet, my toes and I smell the rich river mud. I feel a sense of tremendous strangeness and wonder at being alive. Wonder of wonders! This enlightenment is the nature of all people but, they are unhappy for the lack of it.

So it was that Siddharta Gautama, six years after he left the palace, became the Buddha, the "One who was Awake", known as Sakyamuni, the sage of the Sakyas.

For some time, he continued to sit under the Bodhi tree to enjoy the sense of freedom. He considered teaching, but felt that no-one would want to hear the truth of what he had experienced.

Will people ever be interested in a teaching that undermines their whole sense of existence at the root?

On one hand, he saw the world lost in the pursuit of permanent security, and on the other, saw the subtlety of what he had to teach. Before his quest, however, he had vowed that if he were able to, he would try to alleviate the suffering in the world.

Some people have less attachment than others, so I must speak about what I've experienced!

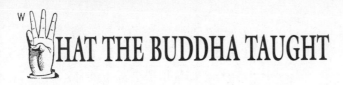 HAT THE BUDDHA TAUGHT

Although we can never be sure of the authenticity of what has been handed down to us as the words of the Buddha, it is clear that there is an essential message common to all traditions. The essence of the Buddha's early teaching is contained in a discourse delivered in the Deer Park at Sarnath in Northern India to his first students. This is now called the Discourse on the Four Noble Truths.

THE NOBLE TRUTH OF SUFFERING

The first of the Four Noble Truths is the truth of suffering.

Suffering is an approximate translation of the Pali word **dukkha**. Dukkha implies impermanence, imperfection and unsatisfactoriness. The Buddha did not start teaching by talking of his enlightenment, of bliss or openness or clarity; he started by talking about the truth of suffering. Many people believe that the Buddha's teaching are pessimistic because of the emphasis on suffering. Representations of the Buddha always portray a radiant and serene appearance, and one of the most common observations about practitioners of Buddhism is that they can combine total seriousness of purpose with a real sense of fun and enjoyment. The Dalai Lama is a good example of this.

Will it last?

How can I hold on to this?

And for many Westerners:

Do I deserve to be happy?

As human beings we all suffer from a fundamental anxiety that creeps into all our activities and makes lasting peace or joy impossible.

I do not deny the existence of happiness. I merely point out that even if we are happy, there is a fundamental anxiety about that happiness.

DALAI LAMA

LIFE'S A BITCH (THEN YOU DIE)

Most of us live without awareness of the natural course of our lives. We were all born but don't remember the pain or shock of the transition from being safe and enclosed to the shock of being pushed out into a new element. We treat illness with resentment as though it is a total betrayal, and our bodies become an enemy. Old age is seen as something that happens to other people, and death is treated like rumour that may or may not be true.

We are all subject to birth, sickness, old age and death, and without an awareness of death, life can only be lived on a shallow level.

The peace and equanimity of the Buddha comes from an acceptance of the transitory nature of life.

Normally, we create goals towards which we are travelling. We hope to achieve ultimate everlasting security and this keeps us continually preoccupied. We are constantly swimming towards what we think is the shore, what we think will be the answer to the problem, whether it be a new love affair, the cure for an illness, a way to stay young or the reward of heaven.

Generally, what we think will be an answer turns out to be the cause of more suffering, so again we look for a solution - the cycle is endless.

The Sanskrit word for this circular chain is **samsara**. Samsaric existence is endless, so long as we live in ignorance.

THE NOBLE TRUTH OF THE CAUSE OF SUFFERING

Suffering begins from basic bewilderment. From that fundamental bewilderment of not knowing who or what we are, we base our perceptions on an idea of ourselves as a permanent entity.

That so-called permanent entity is known as "ego". When we look for this sense of self, there is nothing concrete or real or solid that we can call "me". This leads to constant insecurity. Not seeing the truth of impermanence and egolessness, we suffer because we do not know who we are. The more we cling to the belief in a self, the more pain and alienation we feel.

THE NOBLE TRUTH OF THE END OF SUFFERING

All human beings have experienced glimpses of enlightenment.

Moments when the self-important "I" does not interfere, moments of total immediacy when the mind is not caught up in memories of the past or in daydreams of the future but is totally involved in the present moment – such moments can happen at any time. These glimpses of **nowness** are vivid and give a stark contrast to habitual mind and its struggles.

The end of suffering is **enlightenment, Nirvana!**

All of the Buddha's teachings are a means to experiencing this for ourselves, not as a theoretical exercise but as direct experience.

Enlightenment cannot be described, only experienced.

There is a story that is used to illustrate this point ...

A turtle came to visit a frog who lived in a very small pond.

Where do you come from?

What is the ocean?

I come from the ocean.

The turtle had difficulty in describing the size of the ocean to the frog, whose limited experience was of a very small pond.

There is no way to describe just how big the ocean is.

Finally the turtle has to take the frog to the ocean and the frog is astounded by the vastness ...

The teacher uses all kinds of methods to show the student the vastness of enlightened mind and the absurdity of staying in a small pond. One teacher compared his students to Egyptian mummies who preferred to stay enveloped in bandages rather than be free.

Enlightenment is the total sense of freedom that comes from letting go of the concept of being an individual "self". It is a long journey towards being able to trust that such freedom is possible.

The glimpses of enlightened mind provides the motivation to find a way out of confusion. The Buddha told of a path that ordinary people could travel on to find their own liberation.

THE PATH

The Buddha presented a path that leads to the cessation of struggle and the attainment of enlightenment.

I make no promises and remind you that there is no external saviour. You should rely on yourselves to do what I have done myself.

Since the essence of the Buddha's teaching is contained in the practice of meditation, following the path means a commitment to following that discipline wholeheartedly.

MEDITATION

Meditation is the foundation of Buddhist practice

The practice of meditation was taught by the Buddha 2,500 years ago. It has been the foundation of the tradition since then. It is based on an oral tradition. From the time of the Buddha, this practice has been transmitted from one person to another. In this way, it has remained a living tradition.

In meditation practice, we learn to let go of the thoughts and fantasies that block the direct intuitive experience of who and what we really are. Our constant mental activity is what maintains the illusion of a separate self, and this effort makes us weary.

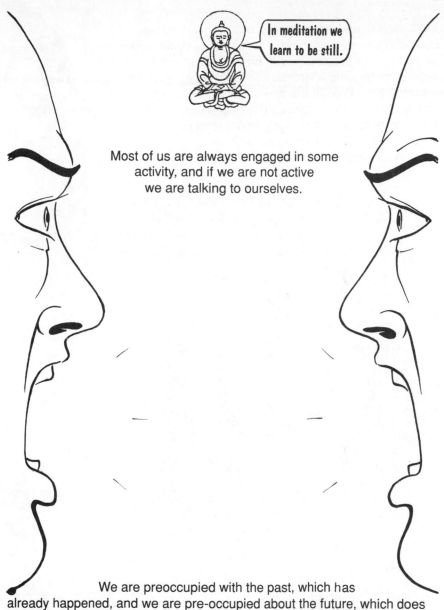

In meditation we learn to be still.

Most of us are always engaged in some activity, and if we are not active we are talking to ourselves.

We are preoccupied with the past, which has already happened, and we are pre-occupied about the future, which does not yet exist. We worry about what will happen and we think about various things that make us feel anxious, frustrated, passionate, angry, resentful, afraid. While we are so preoccupied, our awareness of the here-and-now slips by and we hardly notice its passing. We eat without tasting, we look without seeing and live without ever perceiving what is real.

Meditation practice is not concerned with perfecting concentration, or getting rid of thoughts, or trying to be peaceful. The practice merely provides a space in which we can relate simply with our body, our breath and the environment. Thoughts simply occur within a larger space. In that simple situation, we bring our attention back again and again from fantasy to the simple reality of being in the present moment.

This brings a sense of freedom from the continual whirlpool of thoughts and anxiety, of being chased by our own emotions and sensations. The ability to live in the present moment, rather than in fantasy, allows us to find delight in the world.

The criticism levelled against meditation
that it leads to an unhealthy introspection
is not borne out in practice, for the practice frees
energy which may have been locked up in anxiety.

KARMA

Karma is an Eastern idea that fascinates the West, but is usually misunderstood as fate or pre-destination.

Karma literally means "action" – **it is the law of cause and effect**. Karma is both the power latent within action and the results our actions bring. Each action, even the smallest, will have consequences. To a Buddhist, therefore, every action, thought or word is important and has consequences.

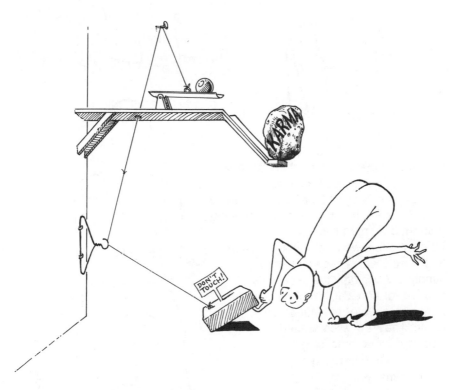

Our present circumstances depend on the result of actions in the past, and our future circumstances depend on actions in the present. Above the individual level, nations have their own particular karma which modifies and changes personal situations.

By seeing clearly how we cause harm to others by our own selfishness, we can take personal responsibility for reducing the suffering in our environment.

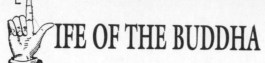

IFE OF THE BUDDHA

The Buddha's first followers were five ascetics with whom he had previously associated. When they first saw him in the Deer Park after his enlightenment, they decided to ignore him because he had given up the life of fasting and austerity.

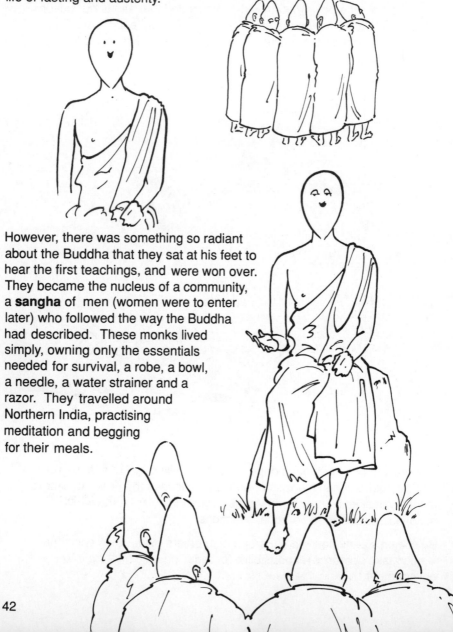

However, there was something so radiant about the Buddha that they sat at his feet to hear the first teachings, and were won over. They became the nucleus of a community, a **sangha** of men (women were to enter later) who followed the way the Buddha had described. These monks lived simply, owning only the essentials needed for survival, a robe, a bowl, a needle, a water strainer and a razor. They travelled around Northern India, practising meditation and begging for their meals.

For the next 49 years, the Buddha walked through the villages of India, speaking in the local language and using themes from everyday life that would be easily understood.

He taught a villager
to practice mindfulness
while spinning cloth,

and when a distraught mother begged him to heal the dead child in her arms, he did not perform a miracle:

Bring me a mustard seed from a house where no-one has died.

She returned without the seed,
but with the realization that death was
universal, and began to follow the path.

During the monsoon season, when travel was difficult, the Buddha and his followers practised meditation. The first retreats were no more than camps, but gradually permanent sites were established as kings and rich patrons donated parks and gardens for retreats.

I accept these gifts but will continue to live as a wandering monk, begging for my meals and spending my days in meditation.

But, as well as meditation, every afternoon after the noon meal, he taught and answered questions from the people who came to hear.

DEATH OF THE BUDDHA

When he was about 80, sensing death was approaching, he gathered his followers together in Kushinagara.

> Arrange a couch for me under the trees.

He lay down on his right side, resting his head on his hand. It is said that at that moment the birds did not utter a sound; the winds ceased to move and the trees shed wilted flowers, which came down like tears.

> I remind you that all things are impermanent - I advise you to take refuge in yourselves and the dharma, the teachings .... Do you have any questions?

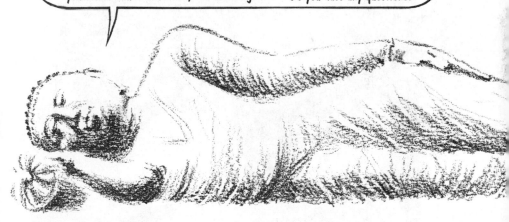

There were none ...

> Everything that is born is subject to decay. Since there is no external saviour, it is up to each of you to work out your own liberation ... These are my last words.

It is said that when he died, the earth quivered like a ship struck by a squall and firebrands fell from the sky. Fearsome thunderbolts crashed down on the earth and violent winds raged in the sky. The moon's light waned and, in spite of a cloudless sky, an uncanny darkness spread everywhere. The rivers, as if overcome by grief, were filled with boiling water. Beautiful flowers grew out of season and over the Buddha's couch, the trees bent down over him and showered him with flowers.

HISTORY OF EARLY BUDDHISM

In the first rainy season after the Buddha's death, the monks and nuns gathered at a mountain cave where they held the First Council. Several of the close followers had memorized what the Buddha had taught them. They repeated it to the whole gathering so that agreement could be established.

These communities had begun during the Buddha's lifetime. At first there were no rules, but gradually certain observances became more established. The rules came about in response to questions asked of the Buddha about specific questions of behaviour. The spontaneous answers turned into rigid and unchanging rules. The following are some of the more obscure rules:

A monk will not put on the inner robe like the trunk of an elephant.

A monk will not go amongst the houses jumping.

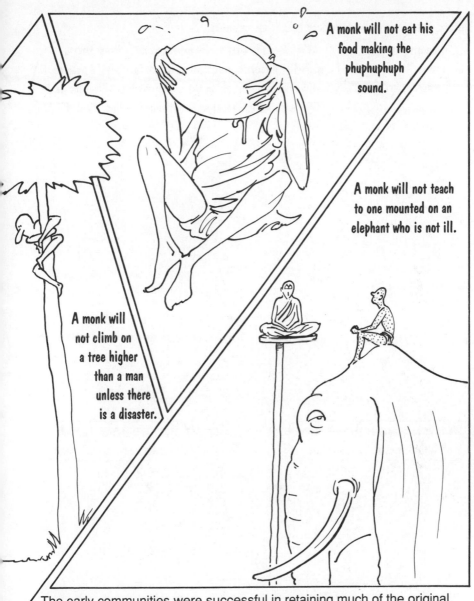

The early communities were successful in retaining much of the original vitality and impetus that had existed when the Buddha was alive. The monastic rules were not the most important feature, and it is recorded that many of the monks and nuns achieved liberation.

The Second Council of the Buddhist community, held about 100 years after the Buddha's death, was the occasion of the first schism.

Before his death, the Buddha has been asked:

Will you give guidance to the community and appoint a successor?

What does the community expect of me? Never having wished to direct it or subject it to my teachings, I have no instruction. I am reaching the end of my life. After my death each of you must work out your own liberation.

The Second Council seems to have been a dispute:

We wish to adhere to the safe course of following established custom!

But changes must be made to meet new circumstances!

Differences in opinion also reflected the development of a strong non-monastic movement within Buddhism which agitated against the monastic elders who had dominated the early sangha. This group of people contributed to the evolution of the Mahayana or "Greater Vehicle" which was open to everyone. The more conservative element survived to the present as the Theravadin School of the Elders, in Southeast Asia.

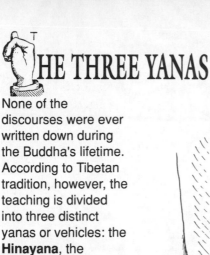

THE THREE YANAS

None of the discourses were ever written down during the Buddha's lifetime. According to Tibetan tradition, however, the teaching is divided into three distinct yanas or vehicles: the **Hinayana**, the **Mahayana** and the **Vajrayana**.

Hinayana literally means "Lesser Vehicle" but it would be more accurate to call it the "Narrow Way". The Hinayana is narrow in the sense that the strict discipline of meditation narrows down or tames the speed and confusion of mind. It allows simple and direct experience of the mind. As well as the discipline of meditation, the Hinayana also stresses the importance of discipline, of being attentive to conduct.

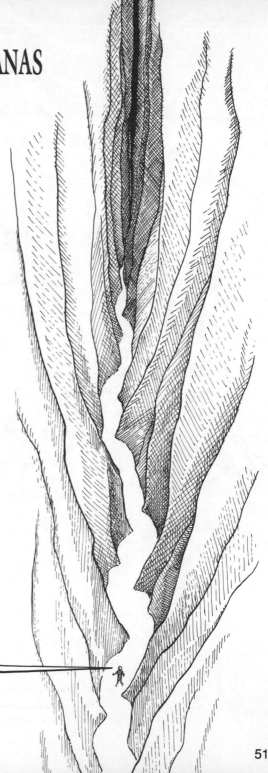

Practising the two disciplines cools down the heat of neurosis. Because of this the practitioner no longer causes harm to himself or others.

The Mahayana or "Greater Vehicle" is like a wide, open highway, in contrast to the narrow path of Hinayana discipline. It goes beyond the Hinayana level of individual liberation alone. Its aim is the liberation of all living beings, which means that everything is included in the vast vision of Mahayana. All chaos and confusion and suffering of self and others is part of the path.

The third yana, the Vajrayana literally means the diamond or indestructible vehicle. The wakefulness of Vajrayana cannot be destroyed because it is recognized as our innate nature.

It is not known whether the Buddha taught all three yanas. What is clear is a continuity of experience running through all the stages, and that they remain remarkably true to the original inspiration of the Buddha's teaching.

Without a proper grounding in Hinayana and Mahayana, it is impossible to step onto the sudden and colourful path of Vajrayana. The relationship of the three stages is depicted in a traditional metaphor. The Hinayana is the foundation of the palace of enlightenment; the Mahayana provides its walls and superstructure; the Vajrayana is its culminating and golden roof – depending on the other yanas for its existence, but providing them with a regal completion. Without a strong foundation in discipline, nothing further can be accomplished.

53

PART TWO
THE MAHAYANA TRADITION

The Mahayana, which arose in the 1st century, is called the Greater Vehicle because its approach opened the way of liberation to ordinary people as well as monks. Seeing themselves as the sole preservers of the word of the Buddha, the monastic community had degraded ordinary householders to the status of mere almsgivers.

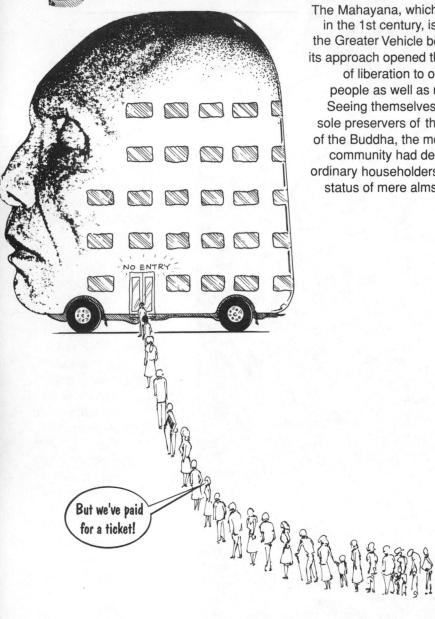

NO ENTRY

But we've paid for a ticket!

The monks were given an opportunity to lead a relatively privileged life, but instead of helping the lay community, began to isolate themselves. Teachings related to meditation and more psychological subjects were taught only among the monks. The Buddha himself had strongly discouraged this inward tendency and had always encouraged his followers to go out into the world. From one of the Buddha's discourses:

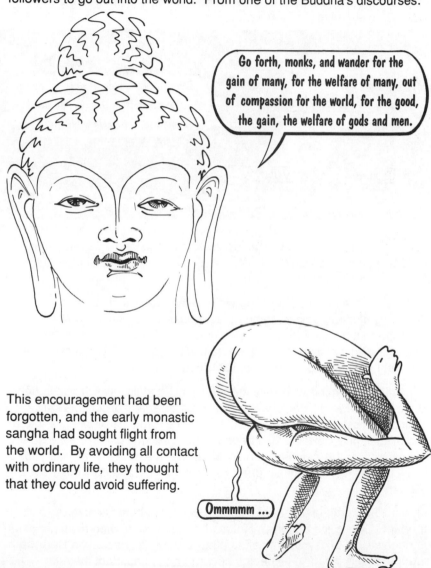

Go forth, monks, and wander for the gain of many, for the welfare of many, out of compassion for the world, for the good, the gain, the welfare of gods and men.

This encouragement had been forgotten, and the early monastic sangha had sought flight from the world. By avoiding all contact with ordinary life, they thought that they could avoid suffering.

Ommmmm ...

HE BODHISATTVA

The followers of the Mahayana returned to the original inspiration of the Buddha to develop compassion for all beings. They felt that the only liberation possible was one in which the experience could be used to further the welfare of others. Individual liberation was impossible if other people were suffering.

Can there be happiness when all living creatures suffer? Can you be saved and hear the whole world cry?

The new ideal became the **Bodhisattva** whose outstanding quality was compassion and who would infinitely delay his or her own enlightenment until all beings were freed.

In this way, the entire world was drawn into the process of liberation. Individual suffering was overcome by a compassion that was so all-embracing that personal sorrow lost its meaning. Paradoxically, if we accept our own suffering and fully relate it with the suffering of others, we transform that pain into a means of liberation.

The ideal of the Bodhisattva transformed early Buddhism which had sought escape from the world, and changed it from a collection of schools – all claiming to possess the true interpretation of the Buddha's teaching – into a world religion in which individual freedom takes second place to a sense of responsibility for the liberation of all beings. Compassion and empathy for one's fellow beings becomes more important than escape from one's own suffering.

To the followers of the Mahayana, the historical Buddha became less important. During the Buddha's lifetime he had been a living example of someone willing to devote himself to others. After his death, the **Buddha principle** that is innate in all beings became more important than the historical Buddha

EXPANSION OF BUDDHISM

Buddhism in India flourished under the patronage of kings and wealthy lay people. In the 3rd century, Buddhism received a tremendous boost by being taken up by the Emperor Ashoka.

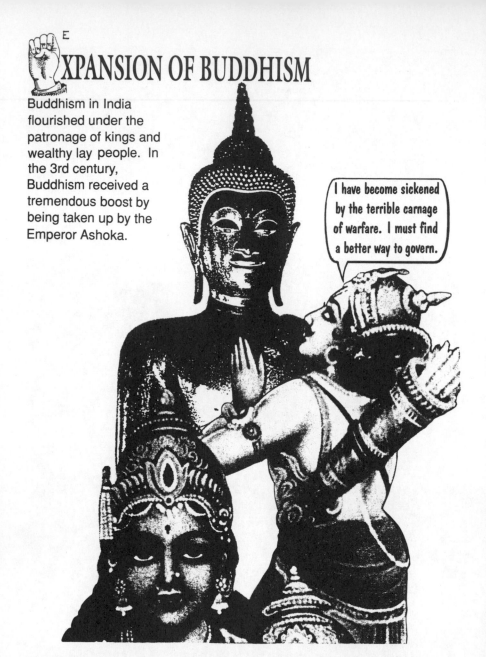

I have become sickened by the terrible carnage of warfare. I must find a better way to govern.

To establish the path of non-violence as a way of life in his empire, he emphasized the Buddhist way of life, social action and compassionate equal justice for all. His rule was outstandingly humane. He set up hospitals for both humans and animals, had wells dug all over India and supported all the different religious traditions in the country.

Ashoka helped to establish Buddhism as a popular religion, where formerly it had been mainly restricted to the educated and privileged classes.

DECLINE OF BUDDHISM IN INDIA

From the 9th century onwards, India was in a turbulent sea of social change and Buddhism declined, mainly due to being incorporated into a new form of devotional Hinduism which had great appeal to the common people.

In the 11th century, the Muslims invaded the country. Those who would not conform to the "One God" of Islam were put to the sword.

By the end of the 13th century, Buddhism had completely vanished from its motherland. However, by this time many of its different schools were firmly established throughout Asia, Tibet, China, Korea and Japan.

STUDY AND PRACTICE OF MAHAYANA

Buddhist texts can appear baffling and obscure. There is a reason for this. Buddhism was never meant to be an object of scholarship alone; the theory was always intended to be accompanied by meditation practice.

A Zen teacher said:

Understanding isn't going to liberate you. Study alone does not provide the power to cut the root of delusion. None of it means a thing until it has been realized - realization comes from the practice of meditation.

Much learning is like a poor man counting another's treasures without a penny of his own.

OINTING THE WAY WITH WORDS

Words are acknowledged as being merely a way of pointing towards the truth. A Mahayana text says:

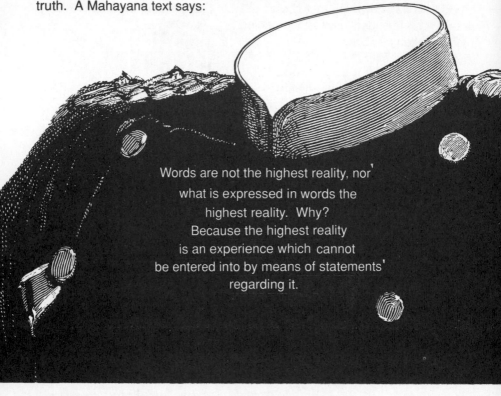

Words are not the highest reality, nor'
what is expressed in words the
highest reality. Why?
Because the highest reality
is an experience which cannot
be entered into by means of statements'
regarding it.

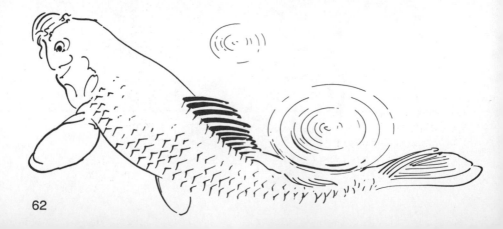

Poetry
and
visual
symbols
come
much
closer
to
reality.

The mind
must be in a state of
wisdom to understand wisdom.

Vast and boundless, nothing is hidden
In clear water, all the way to the bottom
The fish swims like a fish
Vast limitless sky, transparent throughout
The bird flies like a bird
Extremely subtle and profound-
How can I explain?

63

STAGES ON THE MAHAYANA PATH — MAITRI

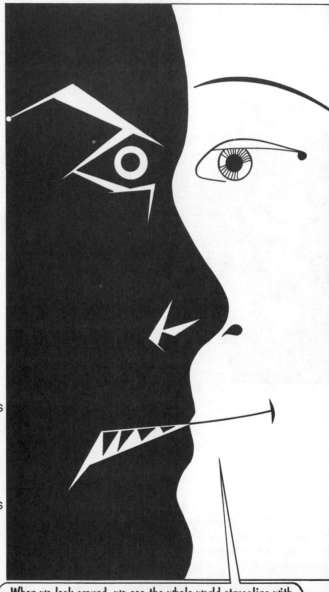

The gateway to practising the Mahayana path is known as **Maitri** or **kindness to oneself.**

The development of maitri comes about when we start to accept negativity as part of the path. We have to make friends with ourselves and be kind to those aspects of ourselves we like least. Learning to be kind to ourselves brings the discovery that fundamentally we are quite soft. We become hard when we habitually deny our own woundedness and blame others for causing our pain. In admitting our own hurt, we become soft and vulnerable.

When we look around, we see the whole world struggling with that vulnerability and tenderness, trying to build solid protection against being touched.

The Mahayana teachings proclaim that all beings possess tenderness, as well as an intrinsic wakefulness which is called Buddha nature.

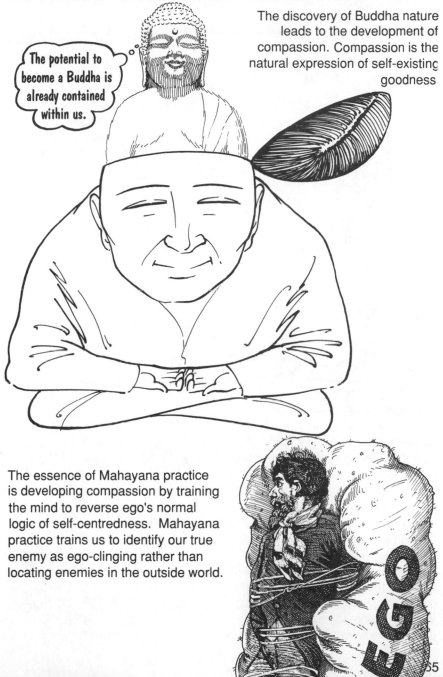

The discovery of Buddha nature leads to the development of compassion. Compassion is the natural expression of self-existing goodness

The potential to become a Buddha is already contained within us.

The essence of Mahayana practice is developing compassion by training the mind to reverse ego's normal logic of self-centredness. Mahayana practice trains us to identify our true enemy as ego-clinging rather than locating enemies in the outside world.

THE ACTION OF A BODHISATTVA

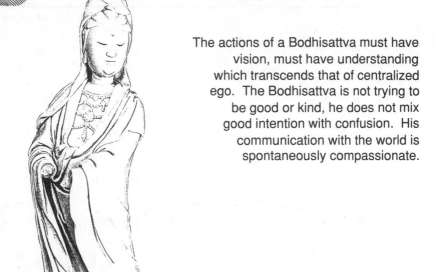

The actions of a Bodhisattva must have vision, must have understanding which transcends that of centralized ego. The Bodhisattva is not trying to be good or kind, he does not mix good intention with confusion. His communication with the world is spontaneously compassionate.

This spontaneous compassion comes from having cut through all conceptualizations by the force of discriminating awareness or **prajna**. Prajna is **fully liberated intelligence**. It does not depend on the confirmation of ego and is traditionally symbolized by a sharp two-edged sword which cuts through all confusion. Prajna cuts through conceptualized versions of goodness, otherwise our version of compassion could be thoroughly aggressive, forcing our kindness down people's throats. Without prajna, the goodness of the bodhisattva would be mere piousness.

Without conscious effort therefore, the Bodhisattva spontaneously helps others. Shantideva, the great 8th century Mahayana teacher writes in his treatise **Entering the Mahayana Path**:

We should become like a bridge that travellers walk over, like moonlight that cools the heat of passion, like medicine that cures disease, or like the sun which illuminates the darkness of ignorance.

SUNYATA

True compassion is the result of experiencing **sunyata**. 'Sunya' means empty; and 'ta' means 'ness'. The doctrine of **emptiness** is the essential teaching of Mahayana. It is the ultimate truth of non-ego.

The experience of **sunyata** occurs as a glimpse of unconditioned mind.

There is no dwelling in past, present or future and one is able to see the world without any pre-conceptions.

It is said that when the Buddha first spoke about sunyata, thousands of his followers died of heart attacks. For the first time, the rug had been completely pulled out from under them. Even though they had been able to see that their own ego was a false construction, what the Buddha said now was that **all** existent phenomena were empty of any self-existence.

All phenomena arise and disappear, all the time constantly changing. No matter what the commonsense view is, if we look closely we can see that there is no solidity anywhere. We have to be content with the realization that this astonishing phenomenon is an appearance that we can neither hold on to nor possess.

The paradoxical nature of reality is expressed in a Mahayana teaching known as the Vimalakirti Sutra. Vimalakirti was said to have been a rich follower of the Buddha who lived a worldly life, yet trod the path of bodhisattva.

The monks were afraid to visit him, because he could always beat them in argument.

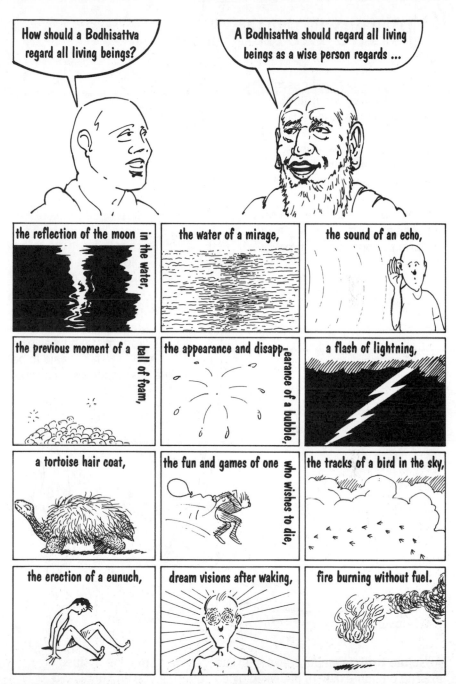

Vivid descriptions of reality, but without substance.

THE TWO TRUTHS

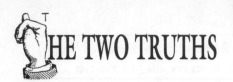

The Mahayana schools describe reality in terms of two truths, **relative and absolute**.

Relative truth is of two kinds. **Perverted relative truth** refers to conventional perceptions in which the world is overlaid with pre-conception and phenomena are seen as solid. This is like mistaking a rope for a snake.

Pure relative truth refers to a direct and simple experience of things as they are, without pre-conception, by one whose perception is free from mistaken views on reality. This is said to be like seeing a rope as a rope.

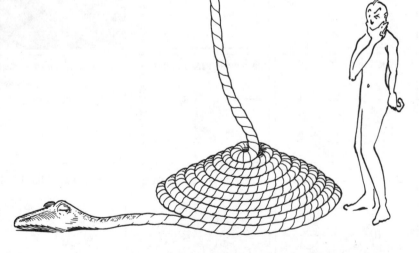

Absolute truth is emptiness, self-existence free from the extremes of existing on non-existing, undefiled by confusion, joyful and unbiased towards pleasure or pain.

MAHAYANA SCHOOLS
THE MADYAMIKA SCHOOL

The Madyamika school was founded by Nagarjuna around the 2nd century AD. In legend, Nagarjuna was taught by the Nagas, water-serpent deities who guard Buddhist scriptures that have been placed in their care because humanity was not ripe for their reception. The important school which Nagarjuna founded put forward no views of its own, but shows in its thousands of texts the self-contradiction inherent in any fixed view about the nature of reality. Wittgenstein and Nagarjuna would have understood one another.

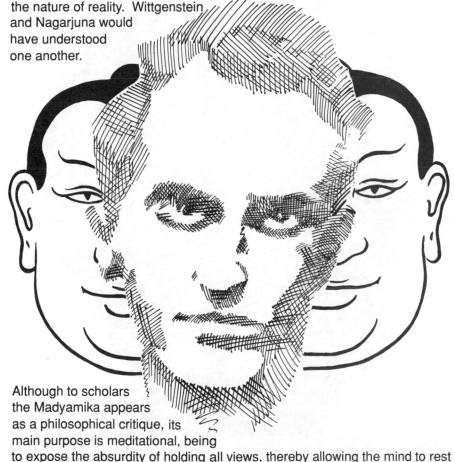

Although to scholars the Madyamika appears as a philosophical critique, its main purpose is meditational, being to expose the absurdity of holding all views, thereby allowing the mind to rest free of all dualistic thought formations. This is the realization of sunyata.

THE YOGACARA SCHOOL

This school, established by two brothers, Asanga and Vasubandhu around the 4th century, holds that all things are reducible to mind only or perception only. Things exist only as processes of knowing, not as "objects"; thus outside the knowing process, they have no reality. The external world is thus "purely mind". According to Yogacara, mind has six kinds of sense consciousness which arise from what is known as the **alaya** or store-consciousness. Jungian scholars see similarities between this and Jung's "collective unconscious".

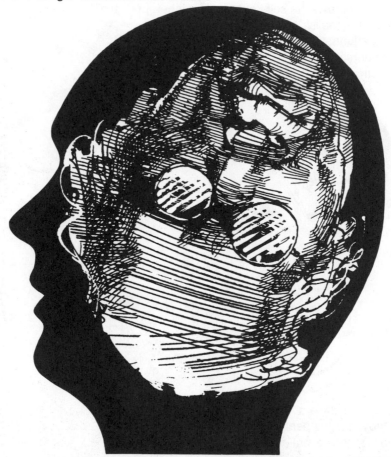

Yogacara was not just a philosophical exercise, however, and is a useful tool in meditation because it emphasizes the immediacy of experience.

EXPANSION OF BUDDHISM INTO CHINA

Ancient Chinese legends tell how a Han Emperor sent envoys to India:

Years later they returned.

Thus Buddhism took root in China.

The truth is less simple. Elements of Buddhism filtered into China along the Silk Route from around the 1st century.

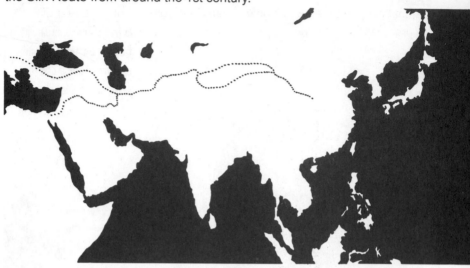

In S.E. Asia, Buddhism had been assimilated into the prevailing cultures with relative ease. China was a different story! It now confronted an unfriendly, ancient and colossal empire, dominated by very clearly defined political and social ideas and customs that had developed over centuries. China felt itself to be superior in every way to neighbouring countries and was not sympathetic to this new barbarian cult with its doctrines of individual liberation.

ONFUCIANISM

Confucianism upheld the ideal of a stable, harmonious social order in which everyone knew their place. Correct ritual was all important and every aspect of life was subject to clear rules of behaviour. Confucianism was very much a religion of "this" world and its followers instinctively objected to a religion that seemed to encourage the abandonment of worldly ties for the pursuit of vague spiritual objectives.

TAOISM

Taoism, the other great Chinese faith was very different. The Taoists were very un-Confucian in their dislike to the social world, which they considered artificial and dishonest. They advocated a return to simplicity and harmony with the natural world.

Their ideal was 'wu wei', non-doing or non-action, which is not intent upon result and is not concerned with deliberate good works or consciously laid plans. They said that if one was in harmony with Tao, the "Cosmic Way", the answer would make itself clear when action was called for, and then one would not act according to deliberate and pre-conceived ways but according to the divine and spontaneous mode of wu-wei, which is the mode of action of Tao itself.

The irreverent flavour of Taoism is exemplified in the following story called Lao Tzu's Wake, written by Chuang Tzu.

There were three friends discussing life.

The three friends looked at each other and burst out laughing. They had no explanation, and thus they were better friends than before.

Then one friend died. Confucius sent a disciple to help the other two chant his obsequies. The disciple found that one friend had composed a song, while the other played a lute.

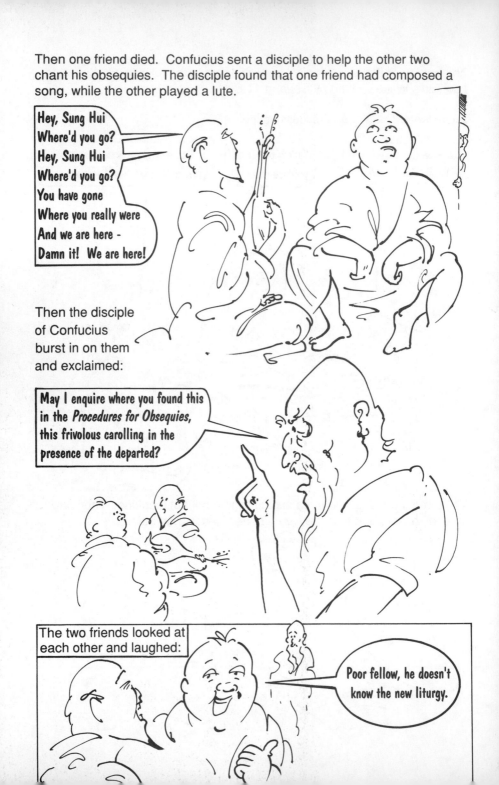

Hey, Sung Hui
Where'd you go?
Hey, Sung Hui
Where'd you go?
You have gone
Where you really were
And we are here -
Damn it! We are here!

Then the disciple of Confucius burst in on them and exclaimed:

May I enquire where you found this in the *Procedures for Obsequies*, this frivolous carolling in the presence of the departed?

The two friends looked at each other and laughed:

Poor fellow, he doesn't know the new liturgy.

The philosophy of
Taoism had much in
common with the
Mahayana spirit
and contributed
humour as a way of
teaching. From the
interweaving of these
two strands, along
with continual
pressure from the
Confucian state,
Buddhism took root
and flowered
in China.

CHINESE BUDDHISM

China is a huge country and during its development Chinese Buddhism took on many forms. As well as incorporating all the Indian Mahayana schools, new distinctly Chinese forms began to develop, some highly disciplined monastic schools and some dealing in magic and sorcery. The Pure Land schools came into being; they were highly devotional and claimed that faith and surrender to the cosmic Bodhisattvas would be the means to salvation.

Some schools have left the myth of the fighting Kung Fu monks.

In a rich display of differing doctrines, Buddhism in China gave rise to extraordinary accomplishments in all its art forms. As early as the 6th century, the immense size of some of the temple complexes was beyond imagination. A third of the capital city, Lo Yan, was occupied by over a thousand Buddhist temples, many of which would dwarf a cathedral and one of the pagodas was an astonishing 200 metres high.

The first printed book that the world had seen was a copy of the Diamond Sutra printed in the 5th century.

The school of Buddhism which had the most influence on the future was the Chan school, later known as Zen.

ZEN BUDDHISM

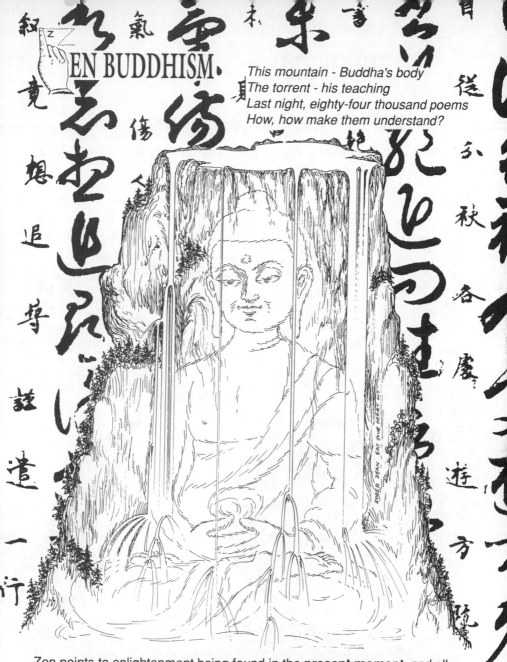

This mountain - Buddha's body
The torrent - his teaching
Last night, eighty-four thousand poems
How, how make them understand?

Zen points to enlightenment being found in the **present moment**, and all of its methods are to wake the student up to the understanding. More than any other school, it stresses the prime importance of the enlightenment experience and the uselessness of religious ritual and intellectual analysis for the attainment of liberation.

ORIGINS OF ZEN

Traditionally, the Buddha himself was said to be the originator of Zen. When he was teaching at Vulture Peak Mountain, several thousand people arrived to hear him talk. He sat in front of them in silence. Time went past and there was still silence. At last, he held up a flower, Nobody understood the gesture except Mahakashyapa, who smiled, having understood that words were not a substitute for the living flower.

He understood the essence of the Buddha's teaching on the spot, and with this, the first transmission from mind to mind took place. This lineage of transmission which began then is of primary concern in Zen, since the authenticity of the enlightenment experience can only be carried out by an enlightened teacher. This direct transmission from teacher to student has kept Zen vital and alive through the centuries.

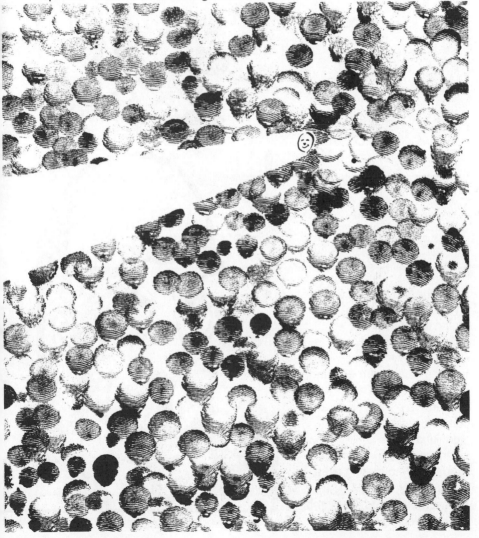

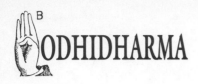ODHIDHARMA

Zen began its rapid growth in early Tang China where it was known as "Chan". The Indian monk Bodhidharma brought Buddhism to China where it began to merge with Taoism, the philosophy that has appealed to poets, painters and mystics for thousands of years.

Bodhidharma was received on his arrival in China by the Emperor Wu, a Buddhist convert, who was very fond of wearing Buddhist robes and reciting chants. The Emperor is portrayed as a cultured, refined aristocrat; Bodhidharma is portrayed as a wild, uncouth barbarian with staring eyes and a bushy beard. He became the 1st Patriarch of Buddhism in China.

Bodhidharma had revealed the essence of his teaching without the Emperor catching on at all.

Bodhidharma wrote a verse which encapsulates the true spirit of Zen:

A special transmission outside the scriptures
With no reliance on words and letters
A direct pointing to the human mind
And the realization of Buddhahood.

Bodhidharma's teaching methods remained essentially Indian in character. It was a later 7th century teacher, Hui-Neng, who gave Zen its characteristic Chinese flavor.

UI-NENG

Hui-Neng came from a poor family, was illiterate and supported himself by selling firewood. One day he heard from inside a house someone reciting from the Diamond Sutra.

Let your mind flow free without dwelling on anything.

Hearing this he had an experience of enlightenment. He learned that the monk who had recited the verse was from the monastery of the 5th Patriarch, Hung-Jen, and decided to go there.

The 5th Patriarch was struck by the young man and immediately recognized his understanding.

The polished, well-read, northern monks at my temple will persecute this illiterate peasant from the south.

Hui-Neng, will you do menial work in this temple?

However, when the time had come to appoint a successor, the 5th Patriarch made a request: I want all the monks to express their experience in a verse.

Shen-Hsui, the head monk and most intellectually brilliant, wrote a poem and submitted it to the community.

The body is the Bodhi tree
The mind is a bright mirror in a stand
Take care to wipe it constantly
And allow no dust to cling.

The verse was much praised but ....

This is polished but rather superficial. I'll write my own verse.

Fundamentally the Bodhi tree does not exist
Nor is there a stand with a bright mirror
Since everything is primordially empty
What is there for dust to cling to?

These two verses illustrate the differences between the northern tradition in China which follows the Indian view of gradual development through constant purification of the mind and the understanding - which Hui-Neng has been the first to articulate - that human beings have Buddha nature which essentially does not need purifying.

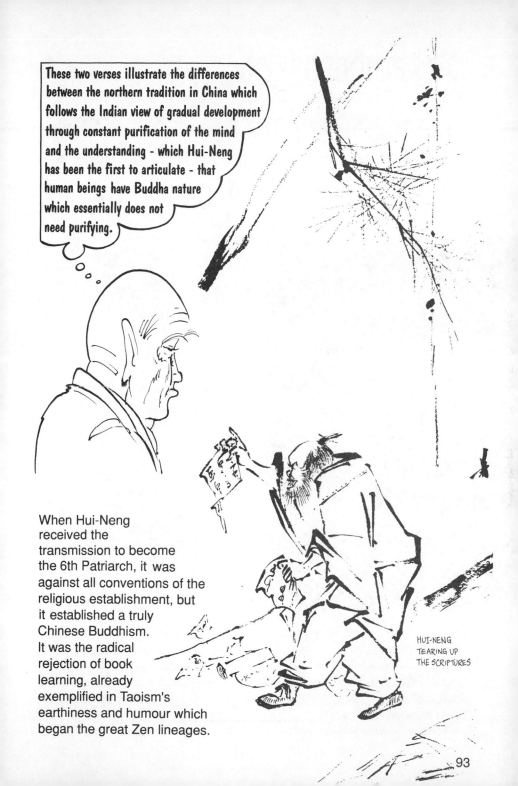

HUI-NENG
TEARING UP
THE SCRIPTURES

When Hui-Neng received the transmission to become the 6th Patriarch, it was against all conventions of the religious establishment, but it established a truly Chinese Buddhism. It was the radical rejection of book learning, already exemplified in Taoism's earthiness and humour which began the great Zen lineages.

ETHODS OF ZEN

Hui-Neng established the two pillars of Zen practice - **Zazen meditation** and **koan study**.

AZEN

OAN STUDY

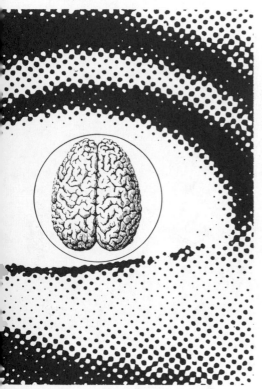

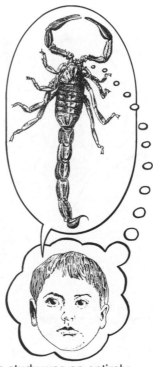

Zazen meditation was essentially similar to techniques taught elsewhere.
It was in Zazen that the intellectual understanding of Buddha-nature could transform into direct personal affirmation of the truth.

Koan study was an entirely new development unique to Zen. A koan is a phrase of the Buddha, a teaching on Zen realization or an episode from the life of a teacher. Each koan points to the nature of ultimate reality. Paradox is essential, as it transcends conceptual or logical thought.

The first koan was a phrase of Hui-Neng. A monk asked him:

We are conditioned to form conceptual answers to questions and it comes as a shock to find there is no answer which fits the question. Koan study is specifically designed to short-circuit the whole intellectual process and experience reality directly.

The answers to koans often seem like witty aphorisms, but to the student absorbed in the koan, the experience is life and death. Some books list the "correct" answers to koans, but without the process of dropping conceptual mind, intellectually knowing the answers is useless.

However, the tradition which had been so alive, became ritualized: every detail of the practice became regularized and koan study became a ritualized formal activity. Around the 10th century, Buddhism in China lost its power; the priests were mainly involved in performing weddings and funerals and exorcising evil spirits. By this time, the living spirit of the tradition had transferred to Japan.

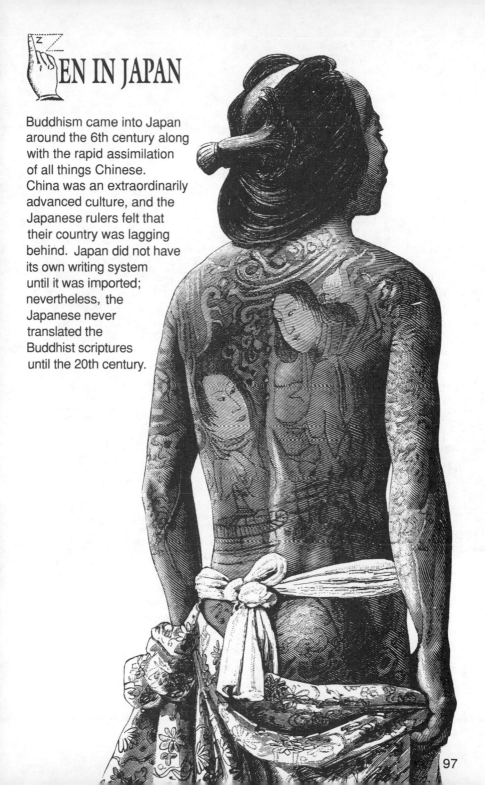

ZEN IN JAPAN

Buddhism came into Japan around the 6th century along with the rapid assimilation of all things Chinese. China was an extraordinarily advanced culture, and the Japanese rulers felt that their country was lagging behind. Japan did not have its own writing system until it was imported; nevertheless, the Japanese never translated the Buddhist scriptures until the 20th century.

Japanese culture had never been interested in other-worldly doctrines; their own indigenous religion was Shinto which was characterized by a belief in a multitude of deities or **kami**. Any mysterious valleys, mountains, rocks, ancient trees, snakes, thunder or fire were regarded as worthy of reverence because they were a connection with the elemental quality of reality. Invoking this elemental quality in which the Kami could enter became part of Japanese character. No part of the daily life was excluded from relationship with the deities - the house had its own kami, the fireplace had its kami - everything that people did formed a connection with the larger world. Abstract speculation about a transcendent realm other than the real world was foreign to Japanese culture.

ZEN TEACHING

Nan-In, a recent Zen teacher met a university professor.

Nan-In, I have come to enquire about Zen.

Sit, professor, and take tea with me.

He served the tea and poured the Professor's cup until it was overflowing. The Professor watched with horror until he could not restrain himself.

Stop pouring - it is overfull!

Like this cup, you are full of your own speculations and opinions. How can I show you Zen unless you first empty your cup?

WHAT IS ONE HAND CLAPPING? THE SOUND OF

Zen adapted to the culture by emphasizing the importance of the "here and now". Zen teaching is always paradoxical and often very humorous. It used examples of ordinary life in the world and turns them on their head. Zen teachers were completely fearless in their attempts to shake their students out of habitual ways of thinking. Their methods were unconventional and sometimes seemingly harsh.

There is a story about a soldier who approached Hakuin, an 8th century teacher.

The General became enraged and began to draw his sword, but Hakuin remarked gently:

The Samurai sheathed his sword and bowed deeply.

Zen practice gave an ability to look death in the face. Most Zen masters wrote death poems as a final message to their students.

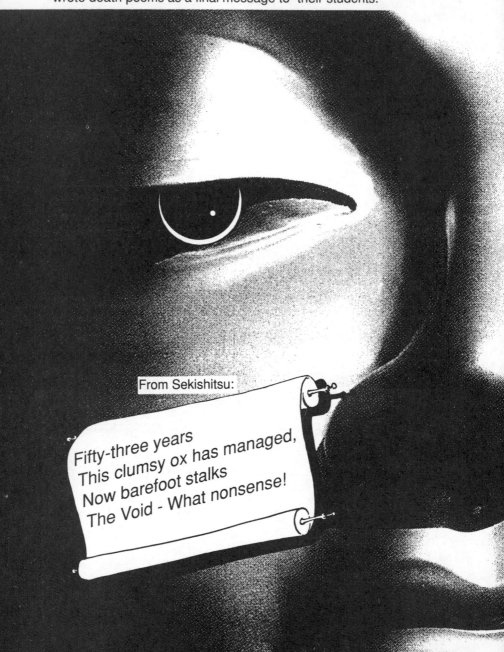

From Sekishitsu:

Fifty-three years
This clumsy ox has managed,
Now barefoot stalks
The Void - What nonsense!

From Daie-Soko:
Life's as we
Find it - death too,
A parting poem?
Why insist?
And from Shozan:
'No mind, no Buddha'
Disciples prattle
'Got skin, got marrow'
Well, goodbye to that.
Beyond, peak glows on peak!

This equanimity in the face of death attracted the samurai warriors to Zen.

Buddhism began to influence the way of warfare, so that victory could be achieved without killing the enemy. The Japanese martial arts are ways to realization; aggression has no part in them.

For example, there is a story about a samurai called Bokuden who was on a small ferry boat with other people.
A swordsman on the boat was bragging:

As the boat reached the shore, he jumped out, took his stance and drew his sword. Bokuden stood up and appeared to follow his opponent but then pushed the boat back into the current. He yelled to the stranded swordsman:

Zen has continued to influence all aspects of Japanese culture up to the present day. Buddhism has not fossilized and is still changing to meet the differing circumstances of a new world order.

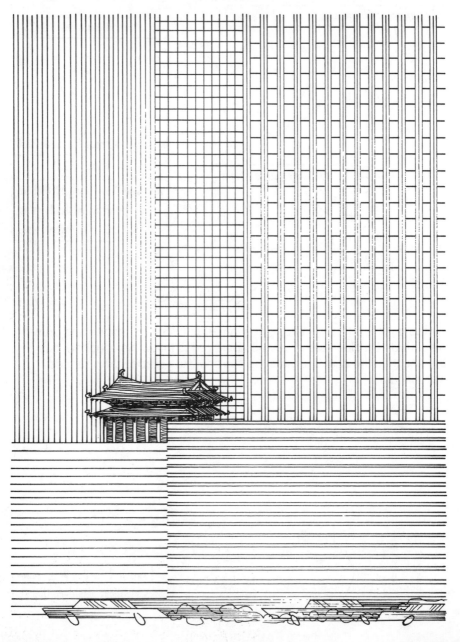

PART THREE

THE THIRD TURNING OF THE WHEEL - VAJRAYANA

Tibet is often called the "Roof of the World" and the Tibetans call their country "The Land of Snows". Most of the country is on a plateau at altitudes of more than 13,000 ft and is surrounded by formidable mountain ranges. The mountains, towering presences high above the world of men, dominate the landscape and have always been considered as the dwelling place of the gods.

BON - THE ORIGINAL RELIGION OF TIBET

The original religion of Tibet was called "Bon". The spirituality of Bon is founded in a cosmological reality; nine gods created the world, a world in which birth, death, marriage and sickness all have their place. If the worshipper can attune himself to the gods through ritual, he can fulfil the cosmic order. By invoking the Bon deities, in the appropriate manner, he can call the gods to himself as allies and defenders.

The Bon gods were as dramatic as the landscape. For instance, Za is the god of psychological energy, lightening and hailstones and causes epilepsy or madness. He is the deity of magicians and is associated with dragons. He rides an angry crocodile and each of his 18 faces is topped by a raven's head that shoots our lightening bolts. He holds a snake lasso, a bag of poisonous water and a bundle of arrows. He has a large mouth in his stomach and his body is covered with eyes.

Early attempts to bring Buddhism to Tibet failed. The Tibetans were very practical, earthy people - mainly farmers - and the Bon system worked for them. Their practice gave them a magical connection with the land they lived on.

BUDDHISM COMES TO TIBET

The rulers of Tibet brought Buddhism to the country, not for religious reasons, but because they wished to acquire the higher culture they saw in adjoining Buddhist kingdoms. In the 8th century, King Trisongdetsen invited the Indian scholar, Santiraksita to Tibet.

Legend has it that evil omens accompanied his stay in the country and he returned to India after several fruitless years in Tibet. Later, a new Indian master was invited; Padmasambhava, the "Lotus-Born".

While Santiraksita had been a conventional monk, a representative of the Hinayana/Mahayana tradition, Padmasambhava was a tantric siddha - one who was accomplished in practising the Vajrayana, or **tantra** as it is also known.

 # AJRAYANA

The Vajrayana is the third turning of the wheel and dates back to the 1st century AD. It is practised mainly in the Himalayan regions, although originally it has been part of the tradition throughout the Buddhist world.

The uniqueness of Vajrayana is the way in which it brings the precise experience of the awakened state into everyday life.

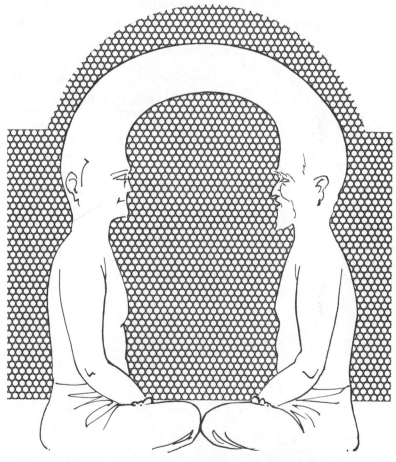

This direct experience of the state of enlightened mind is transmitted by the teacher when the student is open enough to receive it. When the "meeting of minds" or transmission takes place, the student has a direct and undeniable glimpse of the true nature of mind. The teacher introduces and the student recognizes.

The true realization of the nature of mind is only possible when transmitted from the heart of the teacher to the heart of the student.

When that transmission has taken place, you will develop trust - that there is no further need to search for something outside yourself.

As Patrul Rinpoche, a famous Tibetan teacher said:

That's like leaving your elephant at home and going out to look for its footprints.

TRUMPET!

In the Vajrayana, all situations can be used as the spiritual path. The tradition has a rich heritage of people from all walks of life who became enlightened –

scholars,   kings,   pimps,

fisherman,   housewives   and beggars.

The essence of Vajrayana is that any circumstances can be used as a way to wake up. It teaches not to suppress energy or destroy energy, but to transmute it, to go with the pattern of energy. There is no particular clinging even to conventional "goodness" as a reference point.

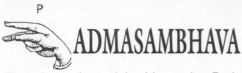

PADMASAMBHAVA

There is a substantial evidence that Padmasambhava was a historical figure. However, as with the Buddha, most of the story of how he introduced Buddhism to Tibet is now highly symbolic.

It is said that Padmasambhava was born miraculously - he just appeared as a beautiful seven-year-old child in the middle of a lotus flower on a lake. Symbolic truth has its own reality; what is being described is the sudden and spontaneous nature of enlightened mind. Its beauty and freshness is suddenly there, without any need to search for it. The suddenness of discovery of enlightenment mind is the essence of Padmasambhava's teaching.

When Padmasambhava came to Tibet, the country was ready for change but many forces in the country opposed the new religion. These forces have become depicted as demons. Perhaps in 500 years, "consumerism" and "scientific secularism" will be characterized in demonic form.

Padmasambhava did not annihilate these forces, however, but subdued them, and made them into guardians of Buddhism in Tibet. Thus many of the terrifying figures in Tibetan art are the old enemies of Buddhism who now act as Protectors. In the West, these demons would have been exterminated in grim witch-hunts, rather than welcomed as protectors.

CRAZY WISDOM

The story of Padmasambhava highlights the way that Vajrayana does not reject anything as a means to liberate people. Vajrayana teachers do not seek to reform their students, but show them how enlightened energy is actually already part of their neurosis. Thus anger can be transformed into sharp intelligence, ignorance into calm equanimity and passion into the warmth of compassion. Whatever the student feels is their biggest failing can be seen as the seed of enlightened mind.

One of the forms that Padmasambhava took was that of the "Crazy Wisdom" guru. In this form he appears as a wrathful figure riding on the back of a pregnant tigress. Crazy wisdom is totally fearless: its power is that it can improvise according to the situation. Fundamentally, that kind of wisdom doesn't hold on to any particular doctrine of discipline. It is totally spontaneous and acts on whatever situation is presented without judgement.

THE SIDDHA TRADITION

Another name of the Crazy Wisdom teacher is "siddha", one who has achieved powers, either magical or spiritual. The siddhas came from all backgrounds; many belonged to lower castes, worked in menial positions and often disregarded the conventions of the more orthodox followers. Every activity could be seen as an expression of Buddha nature and any situation offered an opportunity to cultivate enlightened mind.

Many of the stories of the siddhas begin with a description of someone whose life was in total disarray. The teacher gave instructions which recognized that what may have been the individual's biggest failing could be transformed into an advantage in achieving liberation. Thus a lazy person was given practices which could be done lying down, one who was a habitual liar was given instruction on the falsity of conventional appearances.

Kings, princes, gamblers, drinkers, prostitutes were all given practices that were uniquely suited to their individual needs and circumstances.

TRANSFORMATION OF DESIRE

Pleasure is generally seen as the enemy of spirituality. Tantra's approach is very different. Instead of seeing desire and pleasure as something to be avoided, tantra recognizes the powerful energy aroused by desire as an indispensable resource for the spiritual path. Tantra seeks to transform every experience no matter how "unreligious" it may appear to be.

In Vajrayana there is no value in a spiritual discipline which denies the everyday pleasures of life. It is not the experience of pleasure which is the problem, but the grasping and attachment which puts personal gratification before the needs of others.

SEXUAL TANTRA

The 6th Dalai Lama said:

> If one's thoughts towards the dharma
> Were of the same intensity as those towards love
> One would become a Buddha
> In this very body, in this very life.

Many Westerners, having seen Tibetan art showing deities in embrace, have the mistaken idea that Tibetan Buddhism is mainly concerned with sexual practices. This is far from the truth. The art actually represents the experience of total unity of the enlightened state in symbolic form.

However, sexuality is not rejected and is used as part of the path. For example, one of the siddhas, Bebhaha was described as being intoxicated with sex. His teacher instructed him:

Perceive intercourse as not merely a pleasant interlude, but as spiritual practice of the highest order.

Raise the pleasure beyond pleasure and visualize that pleasure as being inseparable from emptyness.

After 12 years training in this technique, Babhaha attained awakening.

Celibacy is seen as a genuine option for a practitioner. It is not motivated by a disgust for sexuality or aversion to the body, but a genuine recognition of the ability to harness the power of sexual desire. Within Vajrayana, however, if celibacy sours a person, he or she would be encouraged to take a sexual partner.

STAGES ON THE VAJRAYANA PATH

Vajrayana (or tantra as it is also called) is secret teaching. Without a thorough training in meditation, and without a clear motive to help other people, practising tantra is dangerous and ultimately self-destructive. Crazy wisdom without compassion is a deadly combination. Charles Manson, the charismatic leader of a bizarre hippie 'Family' in California, later convicted of the horrific Sharon Tate murders in 1969, was said to have explored some aspects of tantra.

IT's coming down fast

Therefore there are many warnings given to students about becoming a tantric practitioner. The teacher will tell the student:

STORY OF RUDRA

A traditional story is that of Rudra. Rudra was one of two students of a Vajrayana teacher. They went to him and he instructed them in this way:

> Go out into the world and use everything in it, all that is seemingly impure, your emotions, passion, aggression, everything. Transmute all of that. That is the true path of Vajrayana.

Rudra interpreted this to mean he could do anything he wanted.

> I shall go out to start brothels, steal, kill and commit all kinds of harmful actions!

The other student understood that all negative emotions contain wisdom and went away to work on that understanding. After a time they went back to the teacher and described what they had done.

In Tibet to kill one's teacher was seen as the worst crime one could commit.

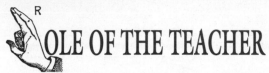

ROLE OF THE TEACHER

In Vajrayana, as in Zen, the teacher is seen as the living embodiment of the Buddha.

> I must be able to demonstrate the living quality of enlightenment to the student, otherwise there will be no genuine transmission.

> I need the example of someone who, while human like myself, has developed beyond the bounds of what I presently believe to be possible.

The student gets a glimpse of the intoxication of being free.

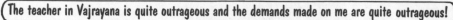

The teacher in Vajrayana is quite outrageous and the demands made on me are quite outrageous!

From all his previous training, the student develops loyalty to the awakened state of mind and realizes that:

I need to submit to the teacher to leave behind all traces of attachment.

This submission is not done from a position of dependence, but is a clear decision based on immense trust.

It is like giving up your life to a good surgeon when you have an illness.

128

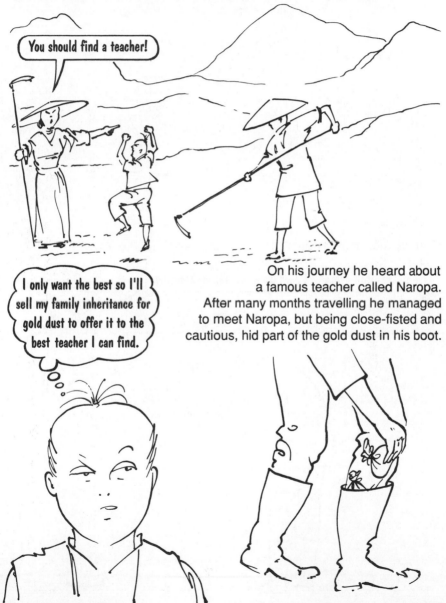ARPA AND MILAREPA

There is a story that illustrates the relationship between student and teacher. Marpa was born into a farming family in Tibet around the 11th century. He was a stubborn and angry child and his family decided:

You should find a teacher!

I only want the best so I'll sell my family inheritance for gold dust to offer it to the best teacher I can find.

On his journey he heard about a famous teacher called Naropa. After many months travelling he managed to meet Naropa, but being close-fisted and cautious, hid part of the gold dust in his boot.

Naropa knew that Marpa was holding back and became angry.

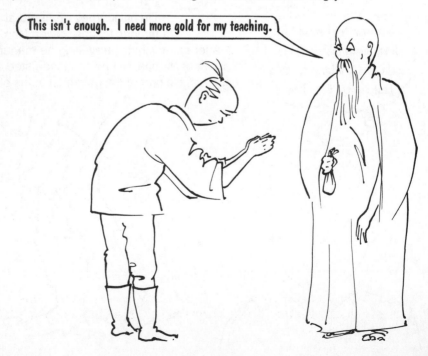

At this point Marpa opened up and was able to receive teaching.

Marpa became a great teacher himself and is seen as the ideal of the married householder who devotes himself to spirituality without neglecting his worldly obligations.

And so it continued ...

After all his ordeals, Milarepa gave up hope. It was at this point of openness that Marpa began to teach him. Some surrender on the part of the student is demanded and any credential must be given up. The teacher is only interested in the student's naked awareness and not in the various masks that the student might wear. The ruthlessness of the teacher in tearing away the student's armour is an essential part of Vajrayana. Whether removal is accomplished wrathfully or peacefully depends on the individual's character.

THE FOUR SCHOOLS OF TIBETAN BUDDHISM

Tibet was unique in that it inherited the whole body of the Buddha's teaching and kept it intact to the present day. Many important Indian texts only exist in Tibetan: the major translation work took place around the 11th century.

Two of the four main schools of Tibetan Buddhism developed around this time, the Sakyas and the Kagyus. The earliest school was the Nyingma School which traced its origins back to Padmasambhava. The last was the Gelugpa school, prominent in Tibet when the Chinese invasion came. The Dalai Lama, as well as being a Gelugpa monk, was also Head of State in Tibet.

In Tibet, one in ten of the male population was a monk. Huge monastic communities grew up like small cities and monks had specialized occupations within the monastery. Priests and teachers were not always monks, many of them were married and supported themselves from a variety of occupations.

VAJRAYANA PRACTICE

According to Buddhist teachings, no matter how confused or deluded we may be at the moment, the essential nature of our being is clear and pure. In the same way that clouds temporarily obscure the sun, so too the temporary negative emotions obscure this clarity.

Experiencing this clarity comes from previous practice. No one can begin to practise tantra without a clear experience of the mind's essential purity. And without a genuine sense of self-worth it would be impossible to have any compassion for anyone else.

According to tantra, perfection is not something that is achieved.

If I practice hard I will become a perfect Buddha

If I behave well perhaps I will go to heaven.

According to tantra, heaven is **now**. We cannot experience this because we hold onto our familiar neurotic small world. In tantra, we are expected to take a leap from limitation into vastness.

The only reason you are daring enough to make the leap is because the teacher had demonstrated that it is possible.

137

VISUALIZATION

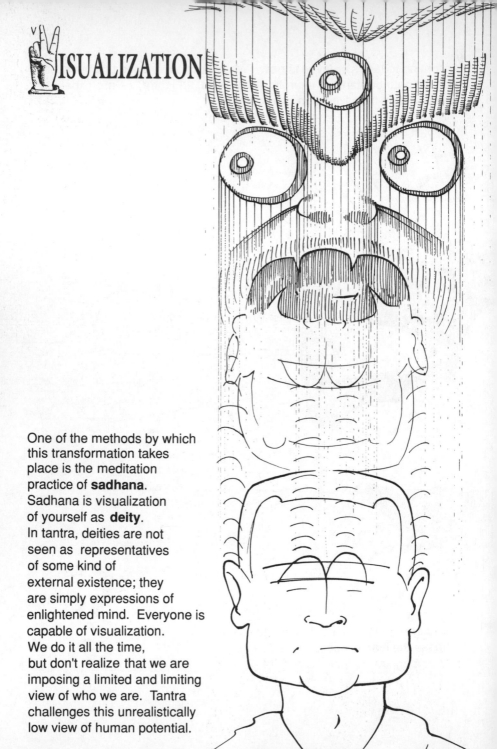

One of the methods by which
this transformation takes
place is the meditation
practice of **sadhana**.
Sadhana is visualization
of yourself as **deity**.
In tantra, deities are not
seen as representatives
of some kind of
external existence; they
are simply expressions of
enlightened mind. Everyone is
capable of visualization.
We do it all the time,
but don't realize that we are
imposing a limited and limiting
view of who we are. Tantra
challenges this unrealistically
low view of human potential.

TANTRIC DEITIES

Tantric deities do not exist in the so called "real world". But nor does Sherlock Holmes or Madame Bovary, even though people may feel very familiar with their characters.

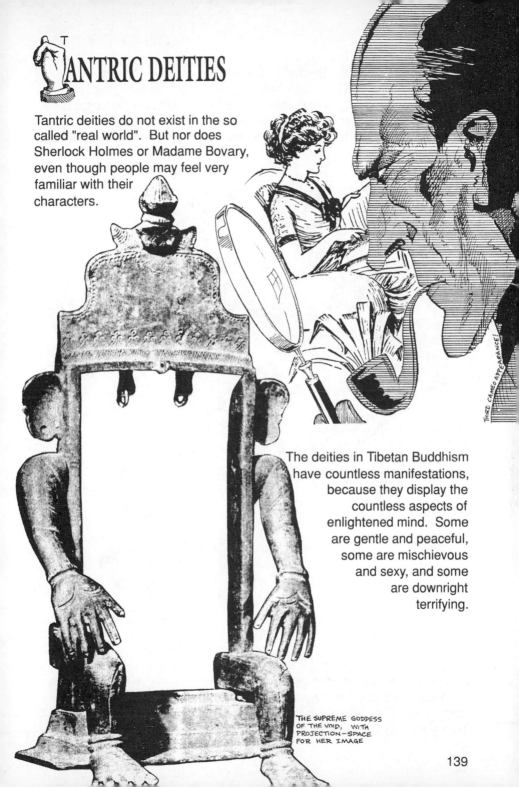

THIRD CAMEO APPEARANCE!

The deities in Tibetan Buddhism have countless manifestations, because they display the countless aspects of enlightened mind. Some are gentle and peaceful, some are mischievous and sexy, and some are downright terrifying.

THE SUPREME GODDESS OF THE VOID, WITH PROJECTION-SPACE FOR HER IMAGE

In sadhana practice, the meditator dissolves all ordinary concepts of himself and becomes the deity. The deity, whether it be terrifying or peaceful, is an archetype of our deepest and fullest nature. In tantra we focus attention on that archetypal image and identify with it. The identification causes a transformation - we no longer see ourselves as limited, dull or foolish, but as having the same attributes as the deity.

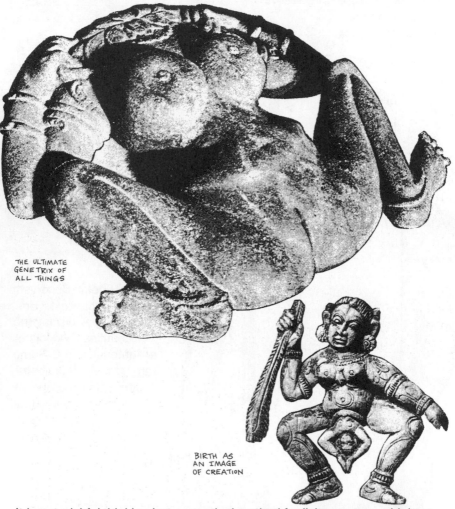

THE ULTIMATE
GENETRIX OF
ALL THINGS

BIRTH AS
AN IMAGE
OF CREATION

It is not wishful thinking but a practical method for living up to our highest potential. The power of creative imaging is only just beginning to be understood in the West. Tibet has much to offer the West in understanding the power of the mind.

TIBETAN BUDDHIST UNDERSTANDING OF DEATH

In the West, there is an intense fear of death. Death is a taboo subject which is hardly discussed. Thus when death is near, the dying person and his or her relatives and friends have no resources to call upon. The process of death has become sanitized. The dead body is put into a clean coffin and taken to a sterile building to be burnt. No one is allowed to see the flames.

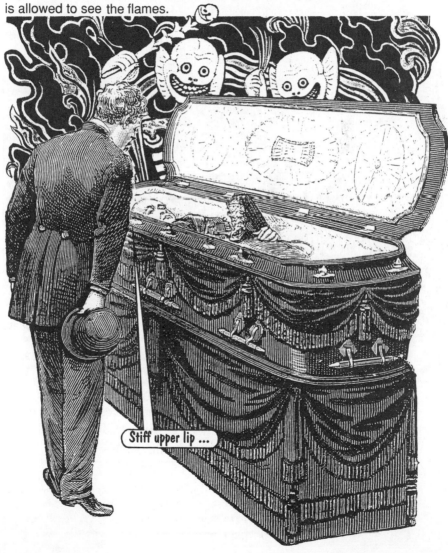

Stiff upper lip ...

In the East, death is familiar. When a person dies, the body is not removed but stays with the family until it is burnt. Family and friends see the body being burned. In Tibet where fuel was scarce, bodies were cut up and left in high open places to be consumed by jackals, wolves, crows and vultures. These cemeteries, or "charnel grounds" as they were known, were terrifying places. The smell of rotting flesh filled the air, parts of bodies were strewn around, hair, flesh, bones, teeth, skulls, fluttering pieces of shroud cloth, as well as the flies and worms and maggots.

It is said that Padmasambhava, after leaving his palace, made a home in the charnel ground. He saw no difference at all between the charnel ground and his palace and took delight in living there. In doing this, he related with death fearlessly.

Since then, many Tibetan practitioners found the charnel ground an excellent place to meditate in, and to this day many ritual instruments are made of human bone.

RITUAL APRON
MADE FROM
HUMAN BONE
FRAGMENTS

Relating with death fearlessly one needs to have no attachment to ego. Our fear of death is the fear of ceasing to exist. The normal routine of daily life ceases to function and you turn into a corpse. The basic fear of discontinuity is the same whether you believe in rebirth or not. Death is the desolate experience in which our habitual patterns cannot continue as we would like them to.

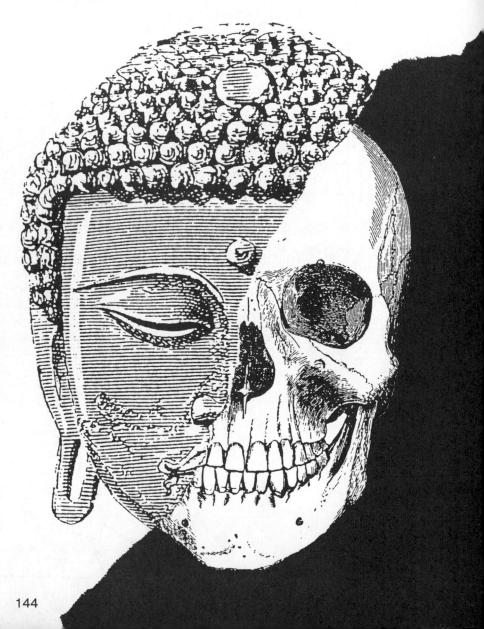

EINCARNATION

The idea that living things are continually reborn was the background to most Eastern thought. Belief in reincarnation existed in early Christianity, and although declared heresy in AD 553, it continued to influence thought in the West.

Buddhists are often thought to believe in reincarnation. This is not strictly true.

Reincarnation presupposes that some kind of enduring soul or essence passes on from one body to another. I deny the existence of a soul that might reincarnate, but I admit something similar which we might call *rebirth*. Rebirth maintains that there is a causal connection between one life and another. The following life is completely new but is conditioned by the old one.

It has been compared to the flame of a nearly spent candle being used to light a new one.

The Buddha himself was unwilling to speculate about what happens after death, because such questions are not useful in the search for reality here and now. Many Westerners become very excited about reincarnation because it gives them a promise of eternal life.

I am reborn!

This seems to be a misunderstanding.

BARDO TEACHINGS - THE TIBETAN BOOK OF THE DEAD

In Tibetan Buddhism there is a detailed analysis of the states that arise between one life and another. This gap is called **Bardo**. Bardo means in-between-state or gap. These states happen all the time, experiences of uncertainty where you are unsure of your ground. This uncertainty or paranoia is strongest at the time of death because you are losing touch with the security and familiarity of having a body. **The Tibetan Book of the Dead** describes the gradual dissolution of the elements at death and the physical and psychical experiences accompanying this. The book is also a text for the living on how to handle chaotic and groundless situations which come up continually in meditation and in daily life.

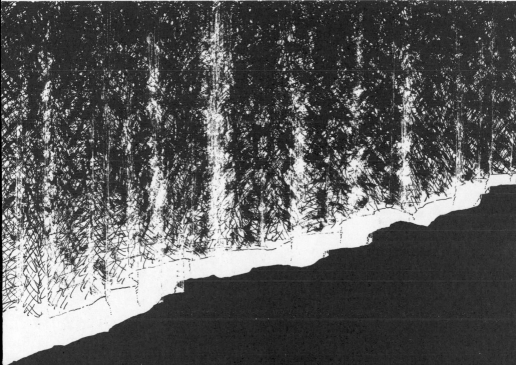

The Bardo describes a succession of experiences, beginning at the moment of death with the experience of a brilliant light. Seeing this brilliance as the true nature of mind, liberation is said to be possible. Usually the dead person's consciousness is too confused to recognize this and is swept on through clear luminous visions, which can be either peaceful or terrifying, towards new rebirth.

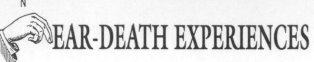

EAR-DEATH EXPERIENCES

There have been many well-recorded stories from people declared clinically dead and then resuscitated. They recall experiences which have remarkable similarities to the descriptions in the Bardo teaching. Most describe a brilliant light of extreme beauty and a simultaneous experience of serenity which transformed their lives afterwards. Many acknowledge a new spiritual dimension in their lives and a lessening of the fear of death.

RELEVANCE OF VAJRAYANA BUDDHISM

Although
Vajrayana Buddhism
seems the most exotic
import to the West,
its flexibility, which
allows it to change
cultural appearance
quickly to meet
new circumstances,
as well as its
complex and profound
insights on human
psychology, make
it well suited to meet
the needs of people
searching for new
meaning in their lives.

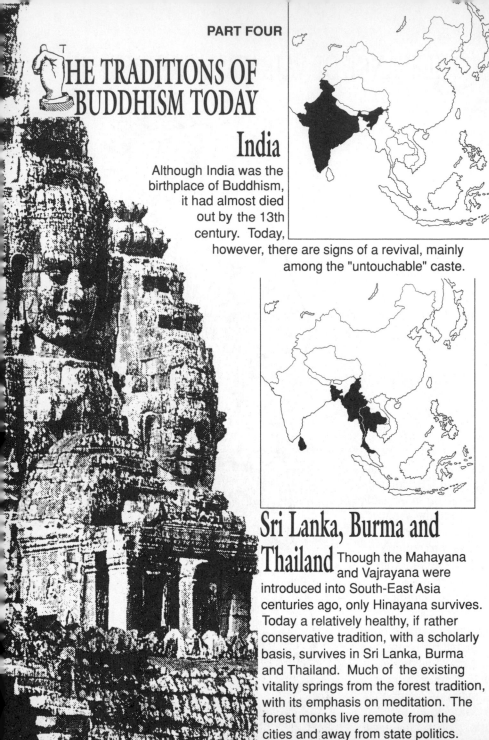

PART FOUR

THE TRADITIONS OF BUDDHISM TODAY

India

Although India was the birthplace of Buddhism, it had almost died out by the 13th century. Today, however, there are signs of a revival, mainly among the "untouchable" caste.

Sri Lanka, Burma and Thailand

Though the Mahayana and Vajrayana were introduced into South-East Asia centuries ago, only Hinayana survives. Today a relatively healthy, if rather conservative tradition, with a scholarly basis, survives in Sri Lanka, Burma and Thailand. Much of the existing vitality springs from the forest tradition, with its emphasis on meditation. The forest monks live remote from the cities and away from state politics.

Laos and Kampuchea

Traumatic political conflicts in Laos and Kampuchea have decimated the Buddhist traditions which had once been so strong. In the "killing fields", the Khmer Rouge dictator Pol Pot exterminated thousands of monks as representatives of the "bourgeois" old order. The future of Buddhism in these countries is highly uncertain.

THE YEAR ZERO

China, Vietnam and Korea

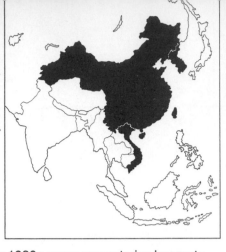

Chinese Buddhism enjoyed immense riches and power in the past, but this led to it becoming a threat to the state. Thus it was outlawed and never fully recovered. The Communist Revolution of 1948 dealt further blows to the ailing remnant of this once glorious tradition. Any kind of renaissance is highly unlikely under the present regime, although during the slightly more relaxed climate of the 1980s some monasteries began to function again.

Chinese influence meant that Buddhism in Vietnam was almost exclusively Mahayana. Buddhism flourished there. One of the most unforgettable images of this century is that of Buddhist monks burning themselves in protest against the imprisonment of thousands of monks by the American-supported Catholic government in power after the French colonialists left. Since 1975, Buddhism has declined and there are stories of persecution.

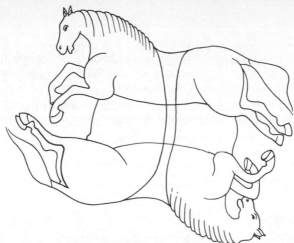

Tibet

Tibet was a unique culture in which Buddhism was harmoniously integrated into every aspect of life. Tibetan culture offered a powerful and coherent alternative to Western egotistical lifestyles. The spiritual, psychological and philosophical insights provided by Buddhism gave rise to a culture where people could feel truly at home on the earth, where loving kindness was normal and where natural resources were honoured.

The Chinese invasion of 1959 was one of the great tragedies of the 20th century. Since 1959, Buddhism has been almost eradicated from Tibet, and because Buddhism was so much in the hearts of the people, the Chinese have made attempts to eradicate the Tibetan nation itself.

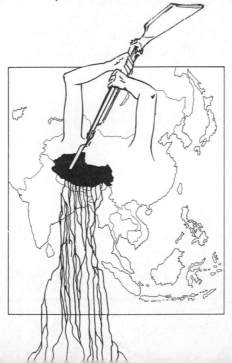

Many Tibetans have become refugees, including their spiritual leader, the Dalai Lama. Despite being spurned by many Western governments, anxious not to lose prospective commercial advantages in China, he has emerged as a world figure and was awarded the Nobel Peace Prize in 1989 for his contribution to world peace. His compassion, patience and kindness, even towards his oppressors, have become a great symbol of the power of Buddhism.

It is hard to predict the future of Buddhism in Tibet, but it seems safe to say that the traditions of Vajrayana Buddhism will continue, perhaps in new forms in the West.

BUDDHISM IN THE WEST

In Tibetan legend, Padmasambhava had said:

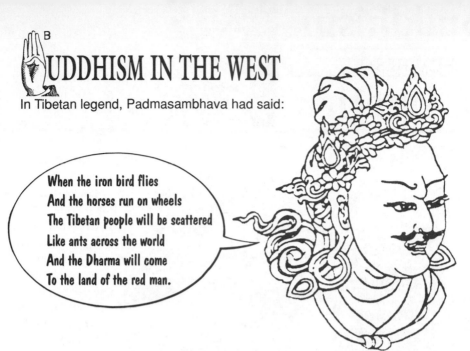

When the iron bird flies
And the horses run on wheels
The Tibetan people will be scattered
Like ants across the world
And the Dharma will come
To the land of the red man.

Although there were early contacts with Buddhism through colonialism, it was not until the 19th century that lasting connections were made. It is ironic that Western imperialism, which tried to impose Christianity on the countries it ruled, became the bridge over which other religions entered the home country.

Buddhism
REACHES OUT
in America

The failure of Christianity to provide real spiritual nourishment has caused many people in the West to explore Eastern religions. At the beginning of the 20th century, many new movements began in Western countries. One of these was Theosophy, which declared that the religions of the world were disintegrated remnants of a great "wisdom tradition" which once existed, and that Buddhism was closest to this tradition. It is doubtful if the Theosophists understood Buddhism, but they introduced it to many people in the West and also encouraged revival in the East.

...estern Hemisphere, is a $25-million, 10-building complex that already is a landmark in Hacienda He...

...oday's gathering of leaders in a Southland temple—the first ...World Fellowship meeting ...tside of Asia—points up a new ...sibility and innovation for the ...religion in the United States.

Photos by
TAMMY LECHNER,
Los Angeles Times

In 1893, the first person from the West formally to become a Buddhist on Western soil was a young Jewish businessman from New York City who had attended the World Conference of Religions in Chicago.

alone:
• The U.S. Defense Depa...
announced that it will allo...

In Britain, Buddhism, generally of the conservative type, remained the interest of a mainly intellectual, middle class elite until the 1960s. In North America, however, the irreverent spirit of Zen was taken up by artists, therapists, musicians and foremost by the poets of the "Beat Generation", particularly Jack Kerouac, Allen Ginsberg and Gary Snyder. Kerouac had a vision in which thousands of young Americans would go on the road as

Zen lunatics ... wild gangs of pure holy men getting together to drink and talk and pray ...

This was in marked contrast to the austerity and discipline of the traditional Zen student.

Drugs gave easy access to altered states of consciousness. Drug takers had visions which had only been available to saints and mystics. All the Buddhist teachers warned that the experiences would be temporary and would not alter the basic ego structure. They admitted that drugs gave a glimpse of other realms, but pointed out the danger of becoming reliant on them, rather than undertaking the discipline that would effect lasting change.

It was in the 60s that Buddhism began to put down roots. People began to practise seriously and find ways to integrate Buddhism into their lives. It stopped being a hobby and became a way of life.

Various Eastern teachers from Japan, Korea, Vietnam, Burma and Tibet were establishing practice centres all over Europe and North America.

BUILDING BRIDGES

Two of the most influential teachers who began teaching in the 60s were Suzuki Roshi, a Zen teacher, and Chogyam Trungpa, a Tibetan lama. Both welcomed and trusted their Western students and displayed a readiness to adapt the traditional forms to meet new and different cultures.

Both teachers were able to bridge the gap between East and West and had a clear vision of what was essentially Buddhist and what was cultural elaboration. They were both able to present Buddhism in a very pure form to the West.

UZUKI ROSHI

Suzuki Roshi loved the West as soon as he arrived.

Buddhism needs some fresh opportunity, some place where people's minds aren't made up.

The fact that his students did not know anything was an advantage, as they had what he called "beginner's mind" which was open and fresh. Zazen meditation was the heart of what Suzuki Roshi taught. Initially he made concessions to his Western students, but gradually they settled in to some very intensive practice.

Suzuki Roshi died in 1971, but the traditions which he established have taken root.

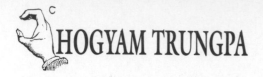

CHOGYAM TRUNGPA

Chogyam Trungpa Rinpoche had begun teaching in England in the 60s where he and another teacher, Akong Rinpoche, had started Samye Ling, the first Tibetan centre in Britain, named after the first monastery to be founded in Tibet by Padmasambhava.

Trungpa Rinpoche had originally been a monk, but found that this created barriers. So in 1969 he gave up the robes and plunged without hesitation into Western life, enthusiastically studying its art, religion, philosophy etc. Only by completely immersing himself in the culture, could he begin to know how to teach Westerners.

His unconventional existence shocked many people in Britain, particularly the old Buddhist guard, and in 1970 be left for America. He immediately appreciated American openness and enthusiasm, but felt that the craze for spirituality in the country was like a spiritual supermarket, the shelves bursting with techniques and gurus. America suffered, he said, from spiritual materialism ...

... deceiving ourselves into thinking we are developing spiritually, when instead we are strengthening our egocentricity with spiritual techniques.

Originally, like Suzuki Roshi, Trungpa made concessions to the Western students, but gradually the discipline increased and his once-wild followers found themselves practising meditation and studying intensively for long periods of time. He established many rural and urban centres, and these have continued to flourish after his death in 1987, following the same training in all three yanas of Buddhism with the emphasis always on meditation practice.

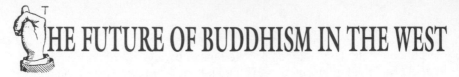

THE FUTURE OF BUDDHISM IN THE WEST

Buddhism has always adapted to new situation. When cultures are experiencing great change, ideas which had previously made sense no longer satisfy and people start to search for new answers. Scientific secularism, which made such changes in improving material conditions of life, has neglected the potential of the human being in favour of what is quantifiable. The West is experiencing a spiritual crisis, and the traditional symbols and doctrines have been dismissed by a scientific world view incapable of providing a satisfactory matrix of meaning. Buddhism is in a good position to be able to provide sustenance in the West.

As it adapts to new cultures, changes will be made and some of the problematic areas have already been identified.

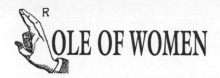OLE OF WOMEN

Traditionally in Eastern cultures, women took a subservient role and this view permeated Buddhism too. In monastic Buddhism a nun was always expected to be deferential to a monk, even a very junior novice.

I am torn between my cultural conditioning and my personal belief that women are equally capable of enlightenment ...

... I'll settle for second-class enlightenment.

There are countless lineage stories of encounters with women which led to a man's enlightenment, but the emphasis is always on the man's story. They give us a tantalizing glimpse of extraordinary women who had overcome the limitations of society; but because history was in the hands of men, their stories are largely unknown.

Buddhism has been preserved in a fundamentally masculine context. Many women are uncomfortable in that environment and, if change does not occur, are prepared to set up new structures which will incorporate more feminine values.

OCIAL ACTION

Suzuki Roshi:

In the East the main effort we make to solve problems is to work inside ourselves. But here in the West, we try to solve problems actively, by action outside of ourselves. The real way to help others should be a combination of the so-called Eastern and Western way.

Many Buddhist centres have now incorporated practical ways of helping others as part of their activity. Many are working in the hospice movement, in prisons, with the homeless, AIDS patients, disturbed people and many other projects.

A Vietnamese teacher, Thich Nhat Hanh has been in the forefront of those involved in social action. One of his most recent projects is working with traumatized American Vietnam veterans. Nearly as many veterans have killed themselves since the war as died in combat. As a Vietnamese, he feels that he is in a unique position to help veterans come to terms with their guilt and anger.

Thich Nhat Hanh has said of his approach to social action:

People often use their anger at social injustice as a basis for action, but that it unwise. When you are angry you are not lucid and you can do harm.

According to Buddhism, the only source of energy that is useful is compassion, because it is safe. When you have compassion, your energy is born from insight, it is not blind anger.

IERARCHY

Many Westerners want the magic of an Oriental teacher. In Eastern Buddhism, surrender to a teacher is an ideal form of practice. The relationship between teacher and student is taken for granted as being the same as that between King and subject, warlord and samurai, boss and employer.

Westerners show little instinct for the kind of obedience and submission that is natural in the East, and while they have been able to accept the authority of an Oriental teacher, when lineages were handed on to Westerners, there was intense resistance to accepting their domination.

The authority assigned to the teacher by the students is based on a shared understanding that the teacher has realized something about the nature of reality that they have not, and that the teacher can therefore guide them to realization better than they can themselves. However, even though students have accepted the teacher's role in cutting confusion, there is antagonism to this and the teacher is often seen as a spokesman of repressive authority.

It will be many years before a happy balance is reached between spiritual hierarchy and democratic ideals.

INTEGRATING WORK AND PRACTICE

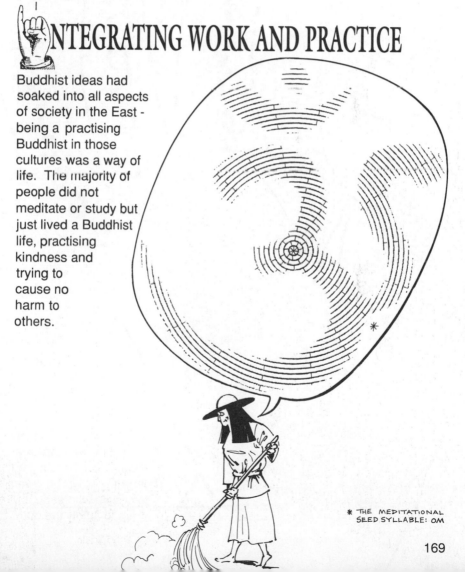

Buddhist ideas had soaked into all aspects of society in the East - being a practising Buddhist in those cultures was a way of life. The majority of people did not meditate or study but just lived a Buddhist life, practising kindness and trying to cause no harm to others.

* THE MEDITATIONAL SEED SYLLABLE: OM

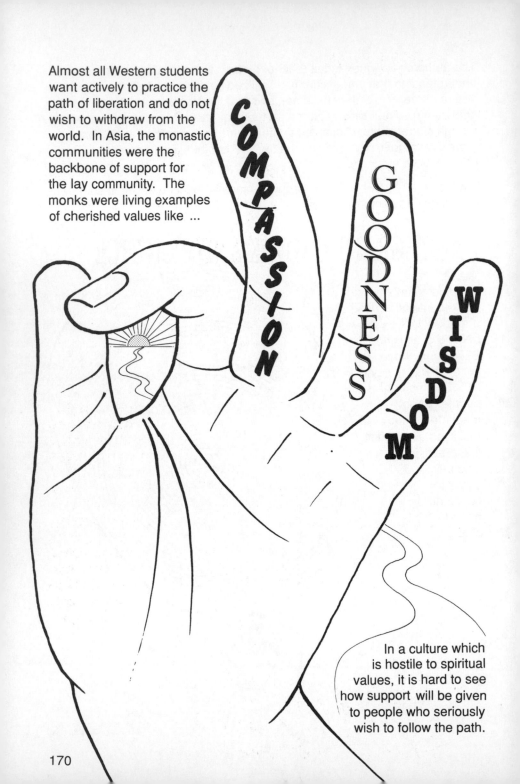

Almost all Western students want actively to practice the path of liberation and do not wish to withdraw from the world. In Asia, the monastic communities were the backbone of support for the lay community. The monks were living examples of cherished values like ...

COMPASSION

GOODNESS

WISDOM

In a culture which is hostile to spiritual values, it is hard to see how support will be given to people who seriously wish to follow the path.

ONCLUSION

Now that Buddhism has begun to take root in the West, those who have survived their first initial enthusiasm are busy trying to cultivate new growth. Western Buddhism is developing its own shape, with an emphasis on community rather than monastery, a re-evaluation of the role of women and attempting to work with hierarchy in a more intelligent way.

Whatever shape it takes, the teaching remains essentially the same as the Buddha proclaimed in the Deer Park at Sarnath. The heart of the teaching remains – the Four Noble Truths, the fact of suffering, its origin, cessation and the path of meditation which puts it all into practice, again and again.

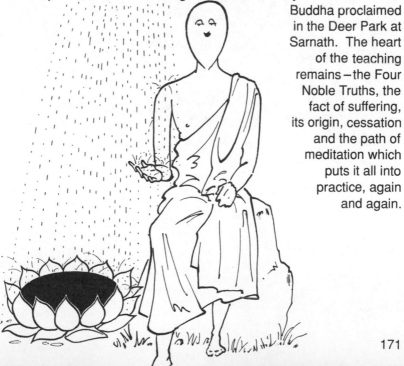

THE SPREAD OF BUDDHISM

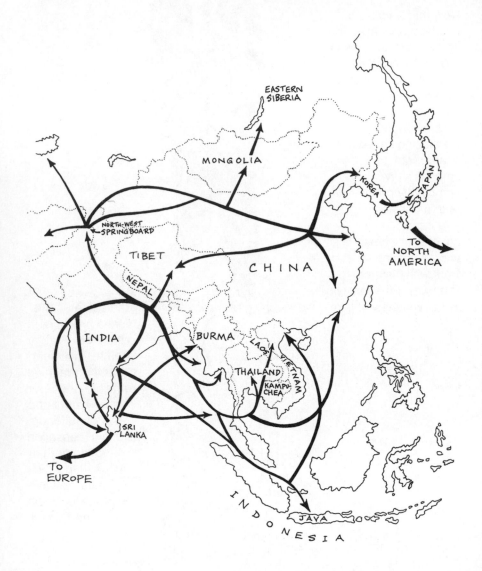

EASTERN
SIBERIA

MONGOLIA

KOREA

JAPAN

NORTH-WEST
SPRINGBOARD

TO
NORTH
AMERICA

TIBET

CHINA

NEPAL

INDIA

BURMA

LAOS

VIET-
NAM

THAILAND

KAMPU-
CHEA

SRI
LANKA

TO
EUROPE

I N D O N E S I A

JAVA

HISTORICAL STRUCTURE

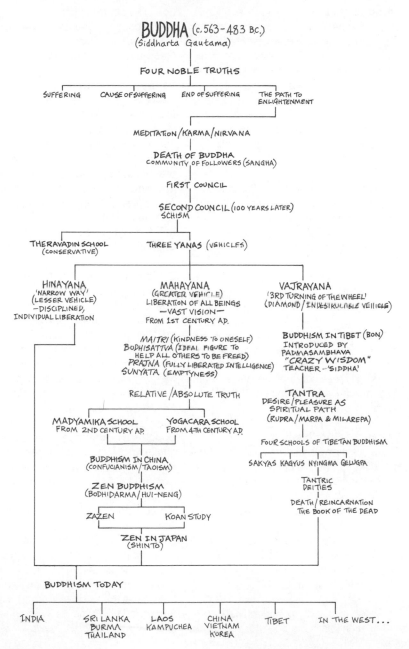

BUDDHA (c. 563 – 483 BC)
(Siddharta Gautama)

FOUR NOBLE TRUTHS

SUFFERING   CAUSE OF SUFFERING   END OF SUFFERING   THE PATH TO ENLIGHTENMENT

MEDITATION / KARMA / NIRVANA

DEATH OF BUDDHA
COMMUNITY OF FOLLOWERS (SANGHA)

FIRST COUNCIL

SECOND COUNCIL (100 YEARS LATER)
SCHISM

THERAVADIN SCHOOL
(CONSERVATIVE)   THREE YANAS (VEHICLES)

HINAYANA
'NARROW WAY'
(LESSER VEHICLE)
—DISCIPLINED,
INDIVIDUAL LIBERATION

MAHAYANA
(GREATER VEHICLE)
LIBERATION OF ALL BEINGS
—VAST VISION—
FROM 1st CENTURY A.D.

MAITRI (KINDNESS TO ONESELF)
BODHISATTVA (IDEAL FIGURE TO
  HELP ALL OTHERS TO BE FREED)
PRAJNA (FULLY LIBERATED INTELLIGENCE)
SUNYATA (EMPTYNESS)

RELATIVE / ABSOLUTE TRUTH

MADYAMIKA SCHOOL   YOGACARA SCHOOL
FROM 2ND CENTURY A.D.   FROM 4TH CENTURY A.D.

BUDDHISM IN CHINA
(CONFUCIANISM / TAOISM)

ZEN BUDDHISM
(BODHIDARMA / HUI-NENG)

ZAZEN   KOAN STUDY

ZEN IN JAPAN
(SHINTO)

VAJRAYANA
'3RD TURNING OF THE WHEEL'
(DIAMOND / INDESTRUCTIBLE VEHICLE)

BUDDHISM IN TIBET (BON)
INTRODUCED BY
PADMASAMBHAVA
"CRAZY WISDOM"
TEACHER – 'SIDDHA'

TANTRA
DESIRE / PLEASURE AS
SPIRITUAL PATH
(RUDRA / MARPA & MILAREPA)

FOUR SCHOOLS OF TIBETAN BUDDHISM

SAKYAS KAGYUS NYINGMA GELUGPA

TANTRIC
DEITIES

DEATH / REINCARNATION
THE BOOK OF THE DEAD

BUDDHISM TODAY

INDIA   SRI LANKA   LAOS   CHINA   TIBET   IN THE WEST...
         BURMA   KAMPUCHEA   VIETNAM
         THAILAND   KOREA

FURTHER READING

Introductory Books
One of the best introductions to Buddhism is an anthology from many different Buddhist cultures, *Entering the Stream*, edited by Samuel Bercholz and Sherab Chodzen, Shambhala Publications, Boston, 1994. Another good introductory book with lots of good pictures is *The World of the Buddha*, ed. Bechert and Gombrich, Thames & Hudson 1985.

Life of the Buddha
Books on the life of the Buddha can be very dull but this one is very readable: *The Awakened One: A Life of the Buddha*, Sherab Chodzen Kohn, Shambhala Publications, Boston, 1994.

Hinayana Buddhism
For a traditional view of Hinayana Buddhism, a good introduction is *What the Buddha Taught*, Walpola Rahula, Grove Press, New York, 1975. For a contemporary view written by a Westerner trained in the Theravada tradition, the following is a valuable guide to meditation: *A Path with Heart*, by Jack Kornfield, Bantam Books, New York, 1993.

Mahayana Buddhism
There are many excellent books on Zen, including the two old classics which inspired the beat generation: *The Way of Zen*, Alan Watts, Penguin, London 1962 and *Zen Flesh, Zen Bones*, Paul Reps, Charles E. Tuttle 1989. Another classic work on Zen describes meditation in a simple and direct fashion: *Zen Mind, Beginner's Mind*, Shunryu Suzuki, Weatherhill, New York, 1971.

For those who enjoy philosophical speculation this is the book for you. If you don't like abstruse philosophy, don't even think about reading it: *The Central Philosophy of Buddhism*, T. R. V. Murti, George Allen and Unwin 1955.

Vajrayana Buddhism
There are countless books on Vajrayana Buddhism. They describe, in detail, once secret rituals and practices but fail to convey to the reader any relevance to modern life. The following two books present the essence of tantra with clarity and simplicity: *Cutting Through Spiritual Materialism*, Chogyam Trungpa, Shambhala Publications, Boston, 1987 and *Introduction to Tantra* by Lama Yeshe, Wisdom Publications, Boston, 1987.

Buddhism in the 20th Century
Two books which give a lively account of how Buddhism is taking root in the West are: *How the Swans Came to the Lake*, ed. Rick Field, Shambhala Publications, Boston, 1992 and *Zen in America*, ed. Helen Tworkov, North Point Press 1989. *Meetings with Remarkable Women*, ed. Leonore Friedman, Shambhala Publications, Boston, 1987 discusses, in interviews with women teachers, the way Buddhism is adapting to meet this challenge. *The Social Face of Buddhism*, by Ken Jones, Wisdom Publications, Boston, 1990 provides an overview of 'engaged' Buddhist social action both in the past and present.

Finally, the most important books are those which tell you where you can go to find out for yourself what Buddhism is all about. Look out for directories and up-to-date news in Buddhist journals available from good newsagents; *Shambhala Sun* and *Tricycle Buddhist Review*.

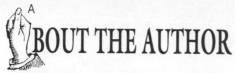BOUT THE AUTHOR

Jane Hope was born in the north east in 1945. After taking a fine art degree she became involved in alternative theatre in the 60 s.

She became a student of the great Tibetan Buddhist teacher, Chogyam Trungpa Rinpoche in the 70 s and was a co-founder of London Dharmadhatu, a Buddhist study and meditation centre.

For the last fifteen years she has lectured and taught meditation extensively in North America and Europe and now works as a Bereavement Counsellor with a cot death charity.

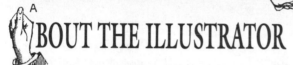

BOUT THE ILLUSTRATOR

At his advanced age **Borin Van Loon**, jobbing illustrator to the bourgeoisie and gentry, really should know better. The Suffolk-based artist and designer has, over the years, freelanced for numerous community and mainstream magazines, has illustrated many books including introductory guides to Darwin and Genetics, and created a bizarre collage comic-strip oeuvre which unfurls as we speak. It is salutary to relate that most common interrogation addressed to him as he reclines amongst florid silken hangings in his spacious air-conditioned studio suite, adorned as it is with priceless Dutch Masters and Magrittes:

When are you going to get a proper job?

Index